IMAGES
of America
GERMAN FLATTS

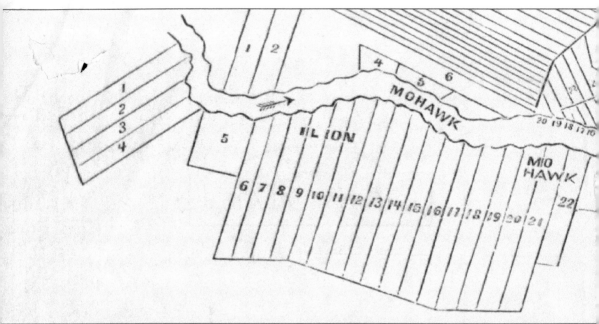

GERMAN FLATTS' EARLY HISTORY. The first settlers in the area of German Flatts were the Palatine Germans who came here in 1723. On April 30, 1725, land that extended from present day Frankfort to Little Falls was granted through the Burnetsfield Patent to 92 persons. The lots on the south side of the river, encompassing the village of Mohawk and Ilion today, were uniform in shape, narrow on the river and extending back 2 miles. The patent holders include Catharina Erghemar (5), Mark Ryckert (6), Apalone Herter (7), Elizabeth Speis (8), Ephraim Smith (9), Godfrey Ruehl (10), Andries Wever (11), Anna Margaret Helmer (12), Delia Korsing (13), Mark Petri (14), Jacob Wever Jr. (15), Mary Feller (16), Rudolph Shoemaker (17), Christopher Fulmer (18), Conradt Fulmer (19), Michael Edick (20), Jacob Edick (21), and Margaret Bellinger (22). (Authors' collection.)

ON THE COVER: Bobsledding down Second Street in Ilion was a favorite pastime. Pictured are some adventurous residents ready to head down the hill on Philo Remington's "Red Cloud" bobsled. (Courtesy of Ilion Public Library.)

IMAGES
of America

GERMAN FLATTS

Susan R. Perkins and Caryl A. Hopson

ARCADIA
PUBLISHING

Published by Arcadia Publishing
Charleston SC, Chicago IL, Portsmouth NH, San Francisco CA

Library of Congress Control Number: 2009939871

For all general information contact Arcadia Publishing at:
Telephone 843-853-2070
Fax 843-853-0044
E-mail sales@arcadiapublishing.com
For customer service and orders:
Toll-Free 1-888-313-2665

Visit us on the Internet at www.arcadiapublishing.com

Dedicated to all of the residents of German Flatts, past and present.

CONTENTS

ACKNOWLEDGMENTS

We would like to thank the following people for helping make this book possible: Lil Gaherty for sharing her knowledge and photographs and for writing our introduction on Mohawk; Jane Spellman for being our liaison with Remington Arms and for writing our introduction on Ilion; Jean Putch of the Ilion Library for always being a ready source of information on Ilion and for making available the well-organized collection of photographs at the library; our volunteers at the Herkimer County Historical Society: Mary Haefele for helping with the research and making many home visits and calls seeking out photographs, Steve Knight for helping research, write captions, and keeping us on track of the landmarks in Mohawk and Ilion, Alta DeLong for sharing her editing and writing talents for our captions, and Betsy Cirelli, Dora Hendricks, Dolores Lyman, Ann Pierce, and Linda Pratt for helping research and sharing their memories of the area; everyone who assisted in finding and who donated pictures for this book: Helen Beauchamp, Marilyn Bridger, Rosemary Williams Brown, Paul Cambridge, Nancy Cioch, Sharon Clapper, Lawrence Clark, Pat Couchman, Tim Daly, Steve Davis, Kathy Durant, Mark Eddy, Lil Gaherty, Ann Casler Green, Frank Spatto and Town of German Flatts, Alice Smallenberger Haefele, Mary Haefele, Jeanette Heath, Jane Hyde, Ilion Public Library (IL), Jane Spellman and Ilion Annunciation Roman Catholic Church, Carol Okusko and Ilion First Baptist Church, Rev. Victor McKusick and Ilion First Presbyterian Church, Rev. Robert Wollaber and Betty Rathbun of the Ilion United Methodist Church, Leslie and Leigh Keno, Ron Keno, Thelma Miles, Mohawk Crowley-Barnum American Legion, Roy Marcot, Sr. Mary Jo Tallman and Mohawk Blessed Sacrament Church, Mohawk Fire Department, Mohawk Homestead, Donna Thompson and Mohawk United Methodist Church, Jack Morrison, Marion Morse, Mary Morse, Sharon Palmer, Nelson Pardee, Joe Putnam, Fred Supry and the Remington Arms Company, Nettie Rix, Lynn Roof, Pamela Shoemaker, Mary Ella Sickler, David Stritmater, Agnes Thomes, Donna Thompson, Pamela Thompson, Weller Library (WL), Jeff Whittemore, and Angela M. Wilson; the following people for sharing information for the book: Sally Baum, Patty Beckwith of Dennison Corners Community Church, Joyce Bradle, Bill Fay, Don Fenner, Nelson Pardee, Agnes Thomes, and Don Urtz. Unless otherwise noted, images in this book are from the authors' collection.

INTRODUCTION

The town of German Flatts came into being even before Herkimer County was laid out in 1791. The towns of German Flatts and Herkimer were established on March 7, 1788. The area north of the river was known as German Flatts and was the site of the Palatine Village settlement. The area south of the river was known for the landholdings of the Herkimer family and Fort Herkimer. Why then is the area north of the river known today as Herkimer and south of the river as German Flatts? When the land was surveyed and a map was laid out noting the location for each town, a misunderstanding between Hon. Simeon DeWitt, then surveyor-general of the State of New York, and Dr. William Petry, a member of the state legislature for Tryon County, led to the famous switch. F. W. Beers' *History of Herkimer County* relates: "The names of *German Flats* and *Herkimer* had been agreed upon, but the location of the two was not understood by the surveyor general. He asked the doctor as to the situation of each. Viewing the ground from his standpoint, below the mouth of the Mohawk, looking up that river, he answered that *Herkimer* was on the left, and *German Flats* on the right. The surveyor-general supposed that the doctor meant the right and left banks of the Mohawk, as the stream flowed; so wrote the names on his maps, and so the error enacted into a law, and the reversal of the names was not known until too late, and so they have remained ever since." The two villages that comprise the town of German Flatts are Ilion and Mohawk.

Can you picture lush green hills on either side of a clear, clean Mohawk River twisting and flowing eastward toward the Hudson? This would be the sight of the northern section of Mohawk, New York, before the building of the Erie Canal.

History saw the French and Native Americans being eventually driven from the territory after heavy losses to the settlers' families, churches, homes, barns, and cattle. The Palatine settlers were able to start all over again. The first settlement in the valley would have been around 1723.

By 1825, the Erie Canal was built, with two locks as well as an aqueduct within the village of Mohawk. The little village began to flourish. Because of the relationship to the Erie Canal, Mohawk became a hub of all types of trading. Farmers carried in grains such as barley and wheat, hops, cheeses, and any other wares to be shipped on the Erie as well as sold or traded in the area of the canal.

There was the need for warehouses along the canal, and many were built. A rolling mill was invented and built right on the canal bank, and this machine mashed grains that had been brought in by local and distant farmers to make malt. The malt was shipped east to make beer (legend says that most of the beer was shipped back to this area).

The village grew by leaps and bounds, and the need for hotels for the overnight canal travelers and traders was in great demand. Mohawk grew to eight hotels and as many grocery stores that carried all kinds of goods. Grocery stores carried yard goods, patent medicines, books, stationery, and whiskey and ale sold by the barrel. There were also grocery stores with a great assortment of supplies located right on the canal as well as in the village.

Packet boats also began to be used to transport people to other villages as well as family outings in other parts of the state.

Naturally, with farmers and other people now being funneled into the area, there arose the need for a cemetery. This in turn created the need for a marble works to make and engrave all kinds of marble. A foundry also became necessary to make the many iron goods that enhanced the new homes and businesses being built.

The population explosion also led to bigger schools and more churches and, of extreme importance, a fire company, which was readily organized and put into action.

Mohawk became an incorporated village in 1844. The first president was Frederick Bellinger.

F. E. Spinner, a local boy, became treasurer of the United States under President Lincoln and built his beautiful home in our village with the first concrete-pipe sewer in North America.

Shortly after the beginning of the 20th century, a beautiful home was given to the village to be used as a library. That library is still used today and will be 100 years old in 2013.

—Lil Gaherty
Village of Mohawk historian

The area now known as Ilion was covered by twelve 100-acre lots beginning at the Mohawk River and extending south as part of the Burnetsfield Patent signed by Gov. William Burnet in April 1725. The lots belonged to women and children and were sold in 1730 to newly arriving families, the Steeles and Clapsaddles. Mills were erected on the creek now known as Steele's Creek to help the few families who settled there.

The Erie Canal went through the area in 1817, and by the time it was finished in 1825, there were a few buildings in what is now Ilion. Eliphalet Remington Jr., whose family settled up the hill in Litchfield, decided in 1828 to bring his forge there to make farm equipment and his famous gun barrels. The original forge used the waters of Steele's Creek; by moving downstream, he could take advantage of the canal for shipping. In addition to manufacturing the barrels (by 1839, Remington was making the whole firearm, lock, stock, and barrel), Remington's agricultural works, started in 1853, eventually manufactured 133 items, from trolley cars to cotton gins. Remington encouraged people to use his forge to make various products; for example, Linus Yale from Newport was making bank vaults and took advantage of the large Remington forge to make vaults, and his son Linus Jr. would invent the key lock. After the hectic days of the Civil War, new product lines began, including the Remington sewing machine (1872), typewriter (1874), and safety bicycle (1892). The growth was gradual enough to use area workers, and there was never a large influx of immigrants in Ilion.

Several other national industries began in Ilion: Library Bureau, making library supplies, would merge with Remington Rand, as did the Remington Typewriter and later Remington Rand's Univac, the first computer company.

The village of 677 residents was incorporated in 1852. There were 68 eligible voters; 57 voted to incorporate, 11 voted no. The name of Ilion was chosen by the postmaster-lawyer James Rasbach rather than Vulcan or Fountain, which had been both put up for a vote. There was a president of the village and four councilmen. At this time, a bank was built as well as a hotel, all backed by Remington money.

Ilion, the largest community in the county in 2009, still has Remington Arms at the center of the village and a healthy variety of businesses and services to make a home for over 8,000 people.

—Jane S. Spellman
Herkimer County Historical Society director, 1974–1995

One

NOTABLE PEOPLE

FRANCIS E. SPINNER.
Francis Elias Spinner
(1802–1890) was born in
Mohawk. He was elected
sheriff of Herkimer
County in 1834 and
oversaw the construction
of the Herkimer County
Jail. In 1838, he was
appointed commissioner
for building the state
lunatic asylum in Utica.
In 1839, he served as
cashier of the Mohawk
Valley Bank, and in 1850,
he became secretary
of the Mohawk Valley
Railroad Company.

TREASURES OF THE UNITED STATES. In 1854, Francis Spinner was elected to Congress, and he served until 1861, when he was appointed treasurer of the United States, serving three presidents, Lincoln, Johnson, and Grant. Pictured is the Committee of Conference of the Senate and House of Representatives on the Army Appropriation Bill on August 18, 1856. From left to right are Sen. William Seward, Congressman Spinner, Congressman Lewis Davis Campbell, Sen. Robert Toombs, Sen. Stephen Douglas, and Congressman James Orr.

TRAILBLAZER FOR WOMEN. As treasurer of the United States, Spinner was faced with the job of increasing staff to produce legal tender. With male employees in the military, he was instrumental in hiring women in the Treasury Department. In 1891, a year after his death, the General Spinner Memorial Association erected a 7-foot, 6-inch statue in his honor; it was brought to Herkimer by the Daughters of the American Revolution and placed in Myers Park in 1909. Pictured with Spinner are, from left to right, Kate Bellinger, Martha Rulison, and Lulu Brown in 1884.

ELIPHALET REMINGTON JR. Eliphalet Remington Jr. (1793–1861) came to the area at a young age when his family settled on a farm on upper Barringer Road in the town of Litchfield. He would make history when he ventured to make his first gun at his father's forge in 1816. His skill led him into the firearms business, and soon the Remington guns became famous and sought after. This popularity prompted the beginning of the Remington Arms Company.

PHILO REMINGTON. Philo Remington (1816–1889) was the eldest son of Eliphalet Jr. and Abigail Paddock Remington. He joined his father's business after graduating from Cazenovia Seminary. He was trained by his father in the use of every tool used in manufacturing firearms, and after his father's death, he took over the manufacturing operations of the company. He and his wife, Caroline Lathrop, built the Remington mansion on Armory Hill overlooking the factory.

PHILO
REMINGTON

SAMUEL REMINGTON. Samuel Remington (1818–1882), the second son of Eliphalet Jr. and Abigail Remington, became the general agent to secure government contracts for the Remington Company. In 1863, he went to Europe to live as sales agent. He returned to the United States in 1877 and resided in New York City until his death. (Courtesy of Remington Arms.)

SAMUEL
REMINGTON

ELIPHALET REMINGTON III. Eliphalet Remington III (1828–1924), the youngest son of Eliphalet Jr. and Abigail Remington, had charge of the office and correspondence for the Remington Company, being noted for his beautiful handwriting. An ardent Methodist, he was always interested in spiritual work and established the *New York Daily Sun* as a means of spreading religious and temperance doctrines. He and his brother Philo donated property for the construction of Syracuse University.

ALBERT N. RUSSELL. Albert Newton Russell (1826–1913) was a noted Ilion businessman. He was one of the receivers of the Remington works upon its momentous failure. Russell started a lumber business and opened the A. N. Russell and Sons cabinet works in Ilion. He was connected in the development of Ilion's water system and in the improvement of village streets and played a large part in the erection of the Ilion Public Library. In 1924, Russell donated land to the village for a park in memory of his father.

DR. HAMBLIN B. MABEN.
Dr. Maben (1833–1912) was one of Ilion's finest doctors. Born in Holcott, New York, he put himself through school and graduated from Albany Medical College at the age of 24. He moved to Ilion in 1860 and started up a practice that specialized in surgeries and obstetrics. He attended over 2,200 births, during which he did not lose a single mother. He died in Kingston, New York, but is buried in the Ilion cemetery.

CHARLES (CARL) MYERS.
Carl Myers (1842–1925) was born in Fort Herkimer and grew up in Mohawk. As a young man, he developed his scientific interests in telegraphy, electricity, and photography. He and his wife, Carlotta, shared a passion for aeronautics and became well known for their balloon ascensions. By 1889, Carl purchased the Gates Manion in Frankfort, where they had a chemical laboratory, machine shops, and a loft to store their balloons. He is noted for his work with the U.S. government involving hydrogen balloons used for meteorology in predicting the weather.

15

WARREN RANNEY. Warren Ranney (1847–1915), with his brother Hiram Ranney (1842–1928), was the inventor and sole manufacturer of the Ranney Brothers' Dustless Ash Sifter, a household article used for sifting ashes from the stove and preventing dust from covering clothes and getting into hair—a good invention for 1876. They set up shop on the Ranney Property in Mohawk on the corner of E. Main and Elizabeth Streets. The business continued until 1886 when the house was converted into a two-family residence.

ARTHUR E. SLOCUM. Arthur Slocum (1855–1928) was born in Ilion and spent most of his life there. As a young man, he worked at the Remington Sewing Machine Works, where he first learned how to engrave. Working freelance, he engraved for jewelers and undertakers until he took a position in Elgin, Illinois, and then Elkhart, Indiana. In 1893, he became a teacher of engraving in the Laporte Watch School in Indiana. It was while at this school that he engraved the English alphabet on the head of a pin. In 1899, he headed back to Ilion and became an engraver for the Remington Typewriter Works. He engraved plates for the cornerstones for the Ilion Masonic Temple in 1908 and the Ilion Odd Fellows Temple in 1911. He and his family lived in a home they built on South Third Avenue in Ilion in 1913.

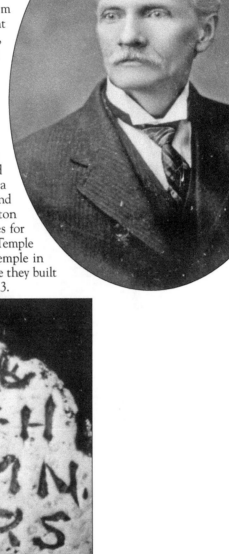

THE STINGY CLUB. The Mohawk Stingy Club was certainly a misnomer. Founded in the 1890s as a benevolent group, the club consisted of about 20 well-known young men of the community. From left to right are (first row) Warren Ranney (1876–1948), William Taft (1861–1917), and Charles Maguire (1876–1911); (standing) William P. Taylor (1876–1929) and Frank Johnson (1873–1903). (Courtesy of Lil Gaherty.)

CIVIL WAR VETERANS. Four Civil War veterans pose on the steps of the Ilion Public Library around 1920. Pictured from left to right are (first row) Theodore Harter (1843–1927), 81st New York Volunteers and William Chandler (1845–1927), Company D, 146th New York Volunteers; (second row) Alonzo Rivers (1838–1941), the last of Ilion's surviving Civil war veterans, who served in the 9th Illinois Regiment after being rejected by local medical examiners and David Wright (1843–1929), Company G, 21st New York Volunteers. (Courtesy of IL.)

MOHAWK DRUM CORPS. The Mohawk Drum Corps, pictured here, was organized in 1903 by William Davis and George Pettingill. This outfit traveled throughout the country and played at the inauguration of Taft and James Sherman. The corps also led Company M of the New York National Guard and paraded at the second inauguration of Theodore Roosevelt. The organization ceased to function shortly after World War I. Pictured in front of the armory building are, from left to right, (first row) George Pettingill, Charles Scott, Morgan Edwards, and Elville Crim; (second row) Harry Maguire, Fred Maguire, William Arthur, and John Crowley; (third row) William Davis, Earl Crim, George Hitcher, John Gora, Don Crim, Delause Dodge, Joseph True, James Maguire, and Joseph Fruteschi. (Courtesy of Ron Keno.)

POLICE CHIEF LOUIS BOWER. A dapper young Ilion policeman models his new uniform around 1895. Though the man is not identified in the picture, it is thought that this is Louis Bower (1867–1922). In 1889, the chief of police became the first uniformed policeman in Ilion. He also served as chief of the fire department and was foreman of the Remington Typewriter Works. (Courtesy of IL.)

POLICE CHIEF WALTER BRONNER. Walter Bronner (1862–1944) was Mohawk's police chief for 35 years, serving from 1902 to 1937. He started out teaching and even working as a cheese maker and a conductor on the Herkimer, Mohawk, Ilion, and Frankfort Street Railway but finally served his community as its well-known police chief. He can be seen here standing in front of the Columbia Street School. Mohawk's municipal building and firehouse, built in 1960, occupy the site today. (Courtesy of WL.)

ALEXANDER HOSE COMPANY. The Mohawk Fire Department posed in their dress uniforms around 1895. The men pictured are, from left to right, (first row) William Lamb, Fred Sayles, and Sam Dennison; (second row) James Gleed, A. J. Moyer, Perry Cress, and Charles Devendorf; (third row) Jerry Warner, Frank Arthur, John Duell, Irving Casey, and Manning Bellinger; (fourth row) Charles Young and Charles Riddell; (fifth row) Ernest Rafter, Frank DuBois, unidentified, Charles Griswold, George Hale, and Richard Winslow; (sixth row) Millard Caple, D. C. Ford, and William Steel. (Courtesy of WL.)

FIREHOUSE ON UNION STREET. Members of Ilion Hose Company No. 1 pose in their firehouse on Union Street in this *c.* 1900 photograph. The village purchased two steamers in 1876, and they served the village until the first motorized vehicles were purchased in 1913. (Courtesy of IL.)

MOHAWK FIRE DEPARTMENT, 1934. Pictured in front of the Rasbach House on Columbia Street are, from left to right, (first row) chief of police Walter Bronner, David Wightman, Mayor Vaughen Guyvits, Earl Palmer, Stewart Monroe, Lewis Dutcher, Chief George Thomes, mascot Delbert Thomes, Victor Smith, Harold Myers, Art Hyde, George Rockafeller, Felix Boon, Al Penner, Lynn Cormon, Harland Schaufler, George Riggs, Harry Thomes, Ralph Cress, and Burton Richardson. In the trucks are, from left to right, (hook-and-ladder truck, left) Alfred Casey, Howard Chambers, Melvin Atkins, Earl Hilts, Floyd Wood, and Henry Loopman; (Ahrens Fox fire truck, center) Douglas Cook, Elmer Miller, Art Helner, and Ray Gleed; (Packard fire truck, right) Leland Steele, James Casey, Ward Decker, and Harry Loopman. (Courtesy of Jane Hyde.)

DR. JENNIE RICHARDSON. Jennie Richardson (1862–1958) was the first female to enter the medical profession in Ilion. She first became a teacher but then followed her passion for medicine when she entered the Woman's Medical College of New York and graduated in 1892. After practicing in New York, she returned to her home in Ilion in 1900 and helped establish the Ilion Hospital, serving as its president for 39 years. (Courtesy of IL.)

BESSIE FULLER. Bessie Fuller (1889–1974) looks like she was everyone's favorite teacher. In 1916, she was appointed second-grade teacher at Mohawk Elementary School, where she taught for 14 years. In 1930, she became principal. In 1951, when Mohawk's Centralized School was opened, combining 13 school districts, she took up combined duties there as principal and second-grade teacher. (Courtesy of WL.)

POLLY JENKINS & HER PALS
Uncle Dan   Texas Rose
                   ILION N.Y.
Heard on COWBOY RECORDS

MARY ZOLLER. Polly Jenkins was the stage name of Mary Zoller (1903–1983), seen here between Texas Rose and Uncle Dan, who was Erlau Wilcox, an Ilion musician. Mary first played the piano professionally at Mohawk's Bates Theater when she was 13. She had a group called Polly Jenkins and her Plow Boys, and during World War II, she entertained on many USO tours. In 1938, the group made a movie with Gene Autry, *The Man from Music Mountain*. (Courtesy of Agnes Thomes.)

MOLLY N. PANCO. Molly (1923–1987) was the first female veteran of World War II in Herkimer County to become a member of the American Legion. She is seen at her acceptance with John Crowley Post No. 25 commander Albert Penner (left) and Adjutant Munson Evans (right) on March 20, 1945. Molly graduated from Mohawk High School in 1941 and, during World War II, served in the U.S. Navy. (Courtesy of the Mohawk American Legion.)

RICHARD GERSTENBERG. Richard Gerstenberg (1909–2002) was born in Little Falls but spent most of his early years in Mohawk, graduating from Mohawk High School in 1928. He went on to pursue a noted career at General Motors spanning 42 years and became its chief executive officer from January 1972 to November 1974. He served on the GM board of directors from November 1960 to May 1980. In 1974, at the Summit Conference on Inflation, Pres. Gerald Ford established a Labor-Management Committee comprising eight distinguished labor leaders and eight distinguished business executives to advise him on major economic policies for the country. Richard Gerstenberg, seen here sitting next to the president at the White House, was one of those distinguished leaders appointed to the committee. He passed away at his home in Paradise Valley, Arizona, at the age of 92.

GREGORY B. JARVIS. Gregory Jarvis (1944–1986) was born in Detroit, Michigan, on August 24, 1944, the son of Bruce and Lucille Jarvis. He came to Mohawk at the age of two. He graduated from Mohawk High School in 1962 and SUNY-Buffalo in 1967 with a degree in electrical engineering. Working as an aerospace engineer for Hughes Aircraft, a company that designed and constructed communications satellites, he was chosen by the company to join a NASA shuttle crew on a mission. Jarvis was bumped twice from missions before he was selected as a member of the crew of the ill-fated space shuttle *Challenger*, which exploded during initial ascent on January 28, 1986. Jarvis is remembered for his constant smile. In February 1986, the Mohawk High School was renamed the Gregory B. Jarvis High School in his honor.

HAROLD E. WHITTEMORE. Harold Whittemore (1915–2001) of Ilion was a well known newspaper man. He published the *Ilion Sentinel*, 1948–1955, and wrote a weekly column, It's the Little Things, for the *Observer-Dispatch* from 1967 until his retirement in 1980 and later for the *Valley Home News*. In his later years, he was the public relations director at Faxton-Children's Hospital. (Courtesy of Jeff Whittemore.)t

CAROL PTASZNIK. Carol Ptasznik of Ilion became the first woman from Herkimer County to graduate from the U.S. Air Force Academy in Colorado Springs on May 28, 1986. She graduated with the rank of lieutenant. June 11, 1986, was proclaimed "Carol Ptasznik Day" in Herkimer County and the village of Ilion in honor of her accomplishment.

LESLIE AND LEIGH KENO. Twins Leslie and Leigh Keno's love for antiques was fostered by their parents, Ron and Norma Keno. After they graduated from Mohawk High School and then Herkimer County Community College in 1977, Leigh went on to Hamilton College and Leslie attended Williams College. Both went on to enjoy successful careers in antiques and collectibles. Leslie joined Sotheby's American furniture and decorative arts department as a cataloguer in 1980 and was appointed director of the department in 1983. Leigh worked as the director of the American furniture department at Doyle Galleries in New York City in 1979 and then became senior specialist of the American furniture department of Christie's. He opened his own gallery in 1986. Their appearances on the popular show *Antiques Roadshow* as appraisers made them household names, and they went on to host their own show, *Find!*, and authored the book *Hidden Treasures*. A highlight of their career was in 2005, when they received the National Humanities Award from Pres. George W. Bush at a White House ceremony. (Courtesy of Leslie and Leigh Keno.)

Two

NOTABLE EVENTS

BOBSLEDDING DOWN WEST HILL. The incline on Second Street in Ilion inspired many an adventurous spirit to bobsled down what was called West Hill. This sport was popular in 1877 and into the early 1900s. Two evenings a week, at a cost of $16 an evening, the Coasting Club had Second Street hill flooded and rutted. As many as 2,000 people would come out and watch the sleds.

MEMORIAL DAY PARADE, 1908. On a nice sunny day in 1908, the Memorial Day parade heads down Otsego Street in Ilion. The home of Dr. Adelbert Douglas is on the far right. Towards the left of the picture can be seen the Civil War monument, dedicated on May 30, 1906, and behind it is the Novelty Works building where the Martin Reel Company was started. (Courtesy of IL.)

GOVERNOR HUGHES VISITS ILION. On October 13, 1908, New York's governor, Charles Evans Hughes, visited Ilion on a tour of the Mohawk Valley. The tour started in Utica and stopped at Ilion, Herkimer, and Little Falls. Hughes was offered the vice presidential nomination on the Republican ticket with William Howard Taft but declined to take the offer. (Courtesy of IL.)

THE BIG FIREMEN'S CONVENTION OF 1914. On the Fourth of July weekend in 1914, the Tri-County Firemen's Convention drew 15,000 people to Mohawk. A big parade made up of 40 organizations, firemen, and musical, civic, and military organizations began the day. Pictured here are a group of firemen marching up Main Street near the corner of Columbia Street. (Courtesy of Lynn Roof.)

MOHAWK FIRE OF 1914. Fire destroyed or damaged a sizable portion of Mohawk's business district on February 13, 1914. The buildings shown here were all built before 1868. The businesses included the Globe Hotel in the center, Joseph Frateschi Confectionery and Fruits to the right, and the Richardson Hardware building on the corner. (Courtesy of Lil Gaherty.)

REMINGTON CENTENNIAL. Ilion held a three-day celebration from August 29 to 31, 1916, to commemorate the 100th anniversary of the making of the first Remington gun. The event opened with the unveiling of a monument at a site in the Ilion Gorge marking the first Remington forge. The next day, Ilion shut its factories down so that everyone could participate in an industrial parade with 10,000 workmen, shown marching up West Main Street in this picture. (Courtesy of Remington Arms.)

NOTED GUESTS OF HONOR. The Remington Centennial in 1916 ended on August 31 with noted guests of honor Sen. Warren G. Harding of Ohio and Maj. Gen. Hugh Scott, chief of staff of the U.S. Army, in attendance. Senator Harding, who would become president of the United States in 1921, gave an address in Monument Square. Pictured are General Scott and his staff parading down West Main Street. (Courtesy of Remington Arms.)

COMPANY M AT WELLER PARK. Company M, based at the Mohawk Armory with their camp set up at Weller Park, had seen five months of guard duty at dams, waterworks, and other public properties throughout New York State. After their sojourn at "Camp Weller," the company was federalized and became part of the 107th Regiment of the U.S. Infantry in 1917.

COMPANY M OFFICERS. Company M officers at Weller Park are, from left to right, Lt. Carey Walrath (1895–1918), Capt. David Wightman (1892–1974), and Lt. Earl Palmer (1887–1970). Walrath and his brother Carleton were killed within seconds of each other in the same shell hole near Bellecourt. Wightman was mayor of Mohawk and was a New York State Asemblyman, serving three terms. Palmer was first commander of the Mohawk American Legion and a 44-year member of the Mohawk Fire Department.

ARRIVAL HOME OF COMPANY M. Thousands of people lined the streets on April 3, 1919, to welcome home the soldiers of Company M who were mustered out of service after World War I. The company joined with the Fourth British Army Corps and served on the front line near Ypres and Mount Kemmel and was part of the attack on the Hindenburg Line.

BIG GATHERING AT THE ARMORY. A parade followed Company M from the New York Central train station in Herkimer to the state armory building in Mohawk, where Congressman Homer P. Snyder of Little Falls, who sent them off in 1917, was there to welcome them home. Of the 162 members who went to war, 26 died in battle and 6 of disease.

FIFTY YEARS OF TYPEWRITER MANUFACTURE. On September 12, 1923, a celebration was held in the village of Ilion to commemorate the day Christopher Latham Sholes, inventor of the typewriter, took his crude machine into the office of E. Remington and Sons and started the manufacture of the Remington typewriter. A bronze tablet was unveiled in honor of the inventor. Pictured above are, from left to right, great-grandchildren Elizabeth and C. R. Sholes; Henry Harper Benedict, Eliphalet Remington III, daughter Lillian Sholes Fortier, and daughter-in-law Mrs. C. G. Sholes. A special drill was performed by the girls who worked at the typwriter factory. (Courtesy of IL.)

GEORGE WASHINGTON BICENTENNIAL. The year 1932 marked a nationwide commemoration of the birth of George Washington. The first president revisited Mohawk on July 21, 1932, at the Shoemaker House, where he had a luncheon 150 years before. About 100 women in Colonial costume took part in the reenactment and little Marion Smallenberger can be seen presenting a bouquet of flowers to the general. (Courtesy of Mary Haefele.)

MEMORIAL DAY PARADE IN WORLD WAR II. The Girl Scouts can be seen carrying the big flag that belonged to the Remington Typewriter Works factory in a Memorial Day Parade during World War II. Leading the girls, at left, is council member Madeline Remmell, and at far right is vice commissioner Ella Dimock. Behind the Girl Scouts are the junior Red Cross girls. (Courtesy of IL.)

PARADE ON WEST MAIN STREET IN ILION. Boy Scouts parade down Ilion's old West Main Street in a show of patriotism around 1944. This picture shows some of the stores that formed Ilion's vibrant business district in the mid-1900s. Starting in the back of the picture are the A&P Supermarket, the Cities Service station, the Home Appliance Store, National Auto Stores, the Powers News Store, and the Thompson gift shop. (Courtesy of Kathy Durant.)

PARADE ON EAST MAIN STREET IN ILION. This is interesting in that it reflects both Mohawk and Ilion in one picture. The photograph shows members of the Mohawk Drum Corps passing by the Remington Arms building on East Main Street in Ilion in 1944. Another interesting note is that this section of Main Street was closed to pedestrian traffic in 1972 and then purchased by Remington Arms from the village for $13,000. (Courtesy of Alice Smallenberger Haefele.)

THE BIG CENTENNIAL CELEBRATION OF 1952. The village of Ilion celebrated 100 years with a weeklong program of activities from June 22 to 29, 1952. Barbara Jarvis was voted Ilion's queen for the week and presided over the events, which included four parades, the pageant *Highlights of Local History*, performed at the Capitol Theatre, inspections of the Remington factories, exhibition shooting, and a whisker contest. Behind this parade shot on West Main Street are the Village Bake Shop, the Statia Shop, and W. T. Grant Department Store. (Courtesy of IL.)

CHILDREN'S PARADE. On June 26, for Ilion's centennial celebration, there was a Children's Parade sponsored by the Ilion Kiwanis Club followed by a children's outing at Russell Park. Pictured are the prize winners in the Children's Parade; from left to right are Shirley Richards, oldest girl's costume; James Green as Tom Sawyer, oldest boy's costume; Ronald Stanburg, most patriotic; Susan Getman, funniest; Christine Wright, prettiest parasol, and Pat and Dick Mooney, oldest couple's costume. (Courtesy of IL.)

THE REBEKAH LODGE FLOAT. On June 27, a Fun Parade, held in the evening, was part of the Ilion centennial. The Violet Rebekah Lodge participated with this float. Pictured from left to right are Wilhelmena Dinga, Mary Ella Sickler, Mildren Dunworth Adams, Marion Wakefield Griffith, Ethel Bluett Gardner, Cora Babcock, Nellie Earnest, and Dorothy Owens. The day also saw the opening of the Herkimer County Volunteer Firemen's Convention. (Courtesy of Mary Ella Sickler.)

CENTENNIAL WHISKER CONTEST. The men of Ilion were a little shaggier this week as they competed in the Remington Whisker Contest. Meredith Minns of Middleville looked the most like Philo Remington and was given the title Mr. Whiskers. After being judged, the men were given a 66 Remington electric razor and had a contest to see who could shave the quickest. Pictured are John Hannahs (left) and Richard Brown. (Courtesy of IL.)

1952 ILION CENTENNIAL EXECUTIVE BOARD. From left to right are (seated) Marie Harter (Miller), publicity; Marceline Carney (Allston), secretary; Bentley Williams, general chairman; Frank Bellinger, treasurer; and Ella Drake Dimock, historical 100 years book; (standing) Ray Baker, Remington Rand; Harry Miller, fraternal; Joseph Baker, schools; Walter Davis, Remington Arms; Walter Weeks, Catholic church; Ted Burkhart, business; Reginald Griswold, Protestant churches; Eugene Stephenson, town; Gordon Rahm, parades; Ray Bennett, village; and Walter VanWiggeren, state. (Courtesy of IL.)

WIND STORM IN FORT HERKIMER. Heavy rainfalls and winds felled trees and ripped roofs off barns on July 18, 1951, in Herkimer County. Residents of Fort Herkimer described it as a twister, with trees down along the sides of Route 5S. Pictured is the Thompson home on Route 5S with crews cleaning up the damage. (Courtesy of Donna Thompson.)

OPPORTUNITY BRIDGE. The bridge leading to Herkimer from Mohawk was known as "Opportunity Bridge" when the Mohawk American Legion would conduct their fund-raising drives by standing on the bridge collecting donations from passersby. Shown are, from left to right, American Legion members Del Thomes, Dick Ludwig, and Paul Cambridge raising funds for the Polio and Heart Fund on January 30, 1960. (Courtesy of the Mohawk American Legion.)

WEST MAIN STREET FIRE IN MOHAWK. In the middle of the night on December 5, 1966, fire swept through the block on West Main Street in Mohawk, destroying Cook's Novelty Store, Lake's Restaurant, Phillips News Store, Zito's Mohawk Home Service Store, and Meyers Pharmacy. Between 15 and 20 families were also left homeless. Located on this site today is the Village Market. (Courtesy of the Mohawk Fire Department.)

WEST MAIN STREET FIRE IN ILION. Fire destroyed two Ilion businesses on May 19, 1973. The National Auto Supply and the Best Supply Company, a hardware store, were completely destroyed as fire swept through the multistory buildings. The Best Supply Company had officially closed its doors the day before and was in the process of moving. The buildings were slated for demolition as part of Ilion's urban renewal project. (Courtesy of IL.)

LIVING HISTORY WEEKEND. Since 2000, the Town of German Flatts has sponsored a Living History Weekend at the end of September. The event is held on the grounds of the town park near the Fort Herkimer Church and features a Civil War reenactment with skirmishes and demonstrations, historical vendors, and tours of the Fort Herkimer Church. This photograph was taken at the event in 2009. (Courtesy of Angela M. Wilson.)

BICENTENNIAL CHORUS. The Mohawk Bicentennial Chorus formed initially to participate in events surrounding the celebration of the nation's bicentennial in 1976. The group came together again in the early 1980s and presented several shows for the community, with proceeds going to assist various local organizations. The chorus was directed by Louise Casey and accompanied by Donald Reardon, both seated in front. Chorus members, many of whom are pictured here, include, from left to right, (first row) Mary Casey, Peggy Hess, Colleen Garlock, Sharon Palmer, Dot Garnsey, Lyn Drury, Monica Peters, Fay Davis, Theresa Casadonte, Esther Milledge, Helen Brandon, and Pat Kelly; (second row) Jane Smithson, Lori Heafey, Theresa Bonfardeci, Donna Thompson, Vicki Baggetta, Marilyn Stone, Rita Mooney, Doris Windecker, Ina Morgan, and Eleanor Stone; (third row) Henry LaRaia, Ed Congdon, P. J. Casadonte, Dean Burt, James Casey, Max Stone, and Walt Walczak; (fourth row) Bill DeCoursey, Bob Brien, Bruce Stone, Ron Cross, Jack Morgan, Norman Stone, Jeff Cross, and Ed Rankins. (Courtesy of Sharon Palmer.)

THE FLOOD OF 2006. The continuous rainfall of the summer of 2006 led to the overflow of creeks and rivers in the Mohawk Valley on June 28. Herkimer County declared a state of emergency. In Ilion, Steele Creek spilled over its banks at the Otsego Street bridge. Mohawk saw the water surge over Fulmer Creek's banks, turning roadways into rivers. Local highways, including the New York State Thruway, were closed, causing traffic difficulties. Areas along the creeks were evacuated. Firefighters from throughout the region came to assist, helping to fight back the floodwaters and working continuously to pump water from local homes. Shelters were set up at the Jarvis Junior-Senior High School, where the Red Cross was based. Pictured are two scenes showing the flood damage in Mohawk. The photograph above shows flood damage to a section of Route 168 (Creek Road), and the one below was taken at the base of Vickerman Hill on Columbia Street. (Both courtesy of Town of German Flatts.)

Three

HISTORIC HOMES
AND BUILDINGS

LIFE IN THE COUNTRY. This spacious farmhouse on Heath Road was owned by John Hawley Heath (1830–1914) and his wife, Anna Shaver Heath (1842–1913). John spent his whole life on the farm, serving his community as a valued member of the Paines Hollow Grange. He is sitting in the chair on the left, and the boy on the horse is his son J. Burton (1881–1941). The woman on the porch is Anna. The two women in front of the fence are unidentified. (Courtesy of Jeanette Heath.)

SHOEMAKER TAVERN. Rudolph Shoemaker was one of the area's original settlers and built this home and tavern in 1768 at what is now 111 West Main Street. It was one of the few structures that was still left standing after the raids through the valley by Joseph Brant, and it is most famous for a visit made by Gen. George Washington on July 28, 1783, on his way to Fort Stanwix. A fire destroyed the building in 1973.

DIEFENDORF HOME. One of the oldest homes in Mohawk that still exists today, it was built in 1778 as a tavern by Judge Gates. In 1804, it was purchased by David Diefendorf and then opened as a "Dutch tavern" until 1842, when it was converted into a dwelling. His son Jacob lived there until his death in 1917, and the house stayed in the family with his daughter Clara Ford. (Courtesy of Jane Hyde.)

FRANCIS E. SPINNER HOME. This Greek Revival brick home that sits at 47 East Main Street in Mohawk is best known as the home of Francis Elias Spinner (1802–1890). Built in 1841, it featured central air and was the first in the United States to have a concrete sewer pipe installed to convey domestic sewage from the home to the Erie Canal, which ran directly behind the house. (Courtesy of Lil Gaherty.)

PETER WARNER HOME. The oldest surviving home in Mohawk is this frame structure at 64 West Main Street built by Peter Warner in 1790. This picture shows Frances Presley, the widow of Harvey Presley. Frances ran a millinery business from the home after her husband's death. The house was later owned by Harry Quayle, who operated an oil business next door. Frances Presley, née Willis, was born and died in this house. (Courtesy of WL.)

CASLER HOMESTEAD. This Greek Revival home was built by Alfred Curtis about 1830 on land purchased from Allen Bennett (from whom the village of Mohawk derived its first name, "Bennett's Corners"). Curtis, of Connecticut, was a carpenter by trade. His daughter, Helen Curtis Marshall, founded the Old Ladies Home. The property was lived in by Josiah Osgood, then Humphrey Root, and for many years, it was the home of Nicholas Casler (1808–1889) and his family. (Courtesy of Jane Hyde.)

CHARLES BENTON HOUSE. Charles Benton (1818–1882) lived in this home, seen on the right at 25 Columbia Street. He was a member of Congress (1843–1847), publisher of the *People's Friend* and *Mohawk Courier* newspapers, and clerk of the state's court of appeals (1847–1853). The home was last owned by Allen and Rosemary Lake, who sold it in 1951 to the U.S. government for Mohawk's new post office; a new building was dedicated 10 years later. (Courtesy of Lynn Roof.)

BROOMHALL MANSION. Located at the apex of Orchard and Michigan Streets in Mohawk, this magnificent home was built by George Broomhall (1812–1890), who came to this country from England and settled in Mohawk. He worked as a maltster, converting grain to malt that was shipped on the Erie Canal to a distillery at Newburgh. About 1840, he built a stone warehouse on the canal bank that was later used by Duofold.

HUMPHREY ROOT HOME. This Greek Revival house at 15 Columbia Street in Mohawk was built around 1835 by Humphrey G. Root (1809–1893). Root and his brother, Elias, ran a general store and cheese forwarding business. Root was employed by the U.S. Treasury under General Spinner and served as canal superintendent and assemblyman. The house was sold in 1900 to Dr. Fred B. Casey (1867–1920). (Courtesy of Jane Hyde.)

REV. JEDADIAH LATHROP STARK HOME. Reverend Stark came to Mohawk in 1842, becoming the first permanent pastor for the Mohawk Reformed Church. He built this Greek Revival home in 1844 at 22 Columbia Street, just two doors above the church. He served the German Flatts area for 20 years. The home was later owned by Robert Glass (1826–1899) and his son Dr. James Glass (1854–1931) and Capt. Andrew Budlong (1843–1929). (Courtesy of Jane Hyde.)

DEWITT ALLEN HOME. Dewitt E. Allen (1851–1933) built this beautiful Victorian house, which still stands at 24 Columbia Street in Mohawk. Allen's father, Enos Allen (1815–1878), founded a furniture store at the corner of Main and Washington Streets in the mid-19th century. Dewitt continued in the business after his father's death until his own death in 1933. A furniture store has occupied that corner ever since. (Courtesy of Lil Gaherty.)

OLD LADIES HOME. This building was purchased in 1895 to provide a refuge for elderly women in destitute circumstances. The effort was spearheaded by Helen Curtis Marshall, who approached prominent women in Herkimer County to take on the cause, raising money to purchase and renovate the large home at 62 East Main Street in Mohawk. This picture is thought to show the staff and residents of the home not long after it was formed. (Courtesy of Mohawk Homestead.)

MOHAWK HOMESTEAD. The first resident of the Old Ladies Home was Sally Howlett. Originally residents were given a lifetime of care by paying a fixed fee and turning over their property, if any. Later residents were charged a fee for each day. By 1991, the home had become an ambulatory care home for adults. The name was changed from the Old Ladies Home to the Mohawk Homestead on January 1, 1967. (Courtesy of Marion Morse.)

SHOEMAKER AND DEVENDORF HOMES. Looking at the corner of West Main Street and North Washington Street in Mohawk in the early 1900s, one sees the brick home of Andrew Shoemaker (1808–1897) and, two houses down, the home of Cornelius Devendorf. Cornelius' son Ralph (1847–1940) fell in love with the girl next door and married Andrew's daughter Florence (1851–1914). They built the house in the middle. (Courtesy of Lynn Roof.)

FLATIRON BUILDING. Every space was utilized when this flatiron building was built at the junction of Otsego and Columbia Streets in Mohawk. The three-story building was owned by Leroy Duddleston in the early 1900s. It was an apartment building in later years, with Alice Brooks as one of the last residents in 1964. It was then torn down and the land made into a small park. (Courtesy of WL.)

FREDERICK WELLER HOME. This brick home at 41 West Main Street in Mohawk is now the Weller Library. Frederick Weller (1819–1911) acquired a fortune through various business enterprises and retired at the age of 38 due to ill health. He purchased this house in 1859 and later purchased six acres south of his home, now Weller Park. After the death of his wife, Helen, in 1912, the house was deeded to the village for use as a library. (Courtesy of WL.)

INTERIOR VIEW. Weller Library was dedicated in 1913. Though modernized where necessary for library purposes, the building has retained much of its original decor and charm. A second-floor museum contains memorabilia of Mohawk's past. Shown is an interior view in the early days of its existence. (Courtesy of WL.)

CROWLEY-BARNUM AMERICAN LEGION. Chartered in 1919 under the name of Lt. Cary J. Walrath; the legion first met in the armory building. The post was renamed John J. Crowley Post 25 in 1934 after a World War I officer killed in action. In 1946, the name of Jamon Barnum, a World War II veteran killed in action, was added and the Fox-Nelson home on Main Street was purchased. Pictured is a Memorial Day service in 1961. (Courtesy of the Mohawk American Legion.)

DOC MORTON HOME. Frank "Doc" Morton, a Spanish-American War veteran, enjoyed sitting in the chair in front of his little two-room house at the bottom of Vickerman Hill in Mohawk at 1 Hammond Street. One of his favorite pastimes was to wave at people as they came off the hill. The home had actually been a gasoline station that he converted into this home and beautiful yard. Nettie and Paul Rix bought the property in 1946 and built a new home here. (Courtesy of Nettie Rix.)

CLAPSADDLE HOUSE. This house at 421 Otsego Street is one of the oldest homes in Ilion. It was built in the late 1700s by William Clapsaddle, who served as supervisor of German Flatts in 1795 and 1798. Peter Clapsaddle, the youngest son, inherited the home. Elsie Whitney, whose mother, H. Gertrude Clapsaddle, was a descendant of Peter, was given this house by her father, Frank Whitney, when she married Carroll Edsall. (Courtesy of IL.)

RASBACH HOUSE. This brick residence was built in 1848 by William Jenks, inventor of the famous Jenks carbine rifle. The Jenks carbine was the first practical breech-loading rifle and brought a business boom to the Remington Armory. The home was sold in 1858 to John Rasbach (1805–1892), a lawyer who was instrumental in incorporating the village and having a road opened to the railroad and establishing a depot. The home was torn down in 1950. (Courtesy of IL.)

THE OCTAGON HOUSE. Harvey Hakes (1831–1915) built this brick octagon house around 1856 at the intersection of Third and John Streets in Ilion with large greenhouses out back. Harvey was a florist for many years with his sons, Seward and George. The house, now stuccoed, originally had a ballroom in the basement along with the kitchen. Harvey was president of the village in 1879 and was one of the developers of West Hill. (Courtesy of IL.)

REMINGTON MANSION. Sitting high atop Armory Hill overlooking the village of Ilion, this three-story mansion was built in 1870 for Philo Remington (1816–1889). It was constructed of pink and grey sandstone, and woodwork in the house was made of hand-carved black walnut. It was fully equipped with bathrooms, kitchens, and a laundry supplied with running water pumped from wells to storage tanks in the house attic. The mansion was razed by Philo's heirs in 1927. (Courtesy of IL.)

REMINGTON STABLES. The building that served as the carriage house and stables for the Remington Mansion estate was purchased in 1927 by the Ilion Little Theatre Club, which converted it into a playhouse. A full season of stage productions has been presented there every year since then. The building, which has come to be referred to as "The Stables," was placed on the National and State Historic Registers in 1976. (Courtesy of David Stritmater.)

CHESTER AND GRACE. In April 1999, the Ilion Little Theatre performed *Chester and Grace.* Pictured from left to right are (seated) David Stritmater, director, and Craig Brandon, author of *Murder in the Adirondacks;* (standing) Norman Turner, Art Wilkes, Nancy Long, Andrea Long, Christine Stegemann, Beverly Poznoski, Robert DeCarlo, John Howard, Jennifer Pokon, Curtis Dulak, Joseph DeLorenzo, Martha Oldfield, Susan Perkins, and John Bullis.

INGLESIDE COTTAGE. In 1888, Thomas Mitchell was the proprietor of Ingleside Cottage, a Victorian home at 78 Second Street in Ilion. It was later owned by Charles Monsell (1858–1926), publisher of the *Ilion News*. It was sold to St. Augustine's Episcopal Church in 1915 to be used as a rectory. The house was moved from the front of the property to the back. It was razed in 1957, when the church bought another home on Otsego Street. (Courtesy of IL.)

DR. HAMBLIN MABEN HOME. This house at 57 Morgan Street in Ilion was the home of Dr. Hamblin Maben, a well-known doctor and businessman. He built the Maben Opera House on First Street in 1870 and also a drugstore and adjoining stores at the corner of First and Otsego Streets. (Courtesy of Tim Daly.)

JOHN HOEFLER HOME. German-born John Hoefler (1829–1905) built this beautiful Italianate-style home on East Main Street in Ilion. John was a toolmaker who worked his way up to superintendent of the Remington Arms Company. He was also one of the incorporators of the Ilion National Bank and the Ilion and Mohawk Gas and Electric Company. The family occupied the home until Elizabeth Hoefler's death in 1915.

WILLIAM BEST HOME. This home on 28 Prospect Avenue in Ilion was purchased by the Presbyterian Church in 1918 as a manse. When the church purchased another home closer to the church property, it was sold to William Best, a church member. Best (1877–1936) was brought to Ilion in 1920 by Remington Arms to be the works manager of the Remington Cash Register Company. (Courtesy of IL.)

ILION FREE PUBLIC LIBRARY. The founding force behind the Ilion Free Public Library was Clarence W. Seamans. Seamans purchased land for the site of the library from Michael Gibblin in 1891. The architect of the Romanesque-style building was George Chappell of New York City, and the builder was Albert N. Russell. It opened on October 28, 1893. (Courtesy of Tim Daly.)

KNIGHTS OF COLUMBUS. Ilion Council No. 518 purchased the former home of John Giblin in 1918. Giblin owned and operated the Giblin Coal Company and helped found the Ilion Savings Building and Loan Association and the Manufacturers National Bank of Ilion. The Council added a hall to the rear of the building. The council was first organized on May 30, 1900, at Harter's Hall. (Courtesy of Tim Daly.)

ILION MASONIC TEMPLE. This photograph is of the dedication of the Ilion Masonic Temple on April 15, 1910. The building's cornerstone of Gouverneur marble, a gift of Br. Frank McKeon of Olive Branch Lodge No. 40 in Frankfort, was laid on October 1, 1908, by Grand Master Samuel Sawyer in the presence of the entire grand lodge. Ilion Lodge F&AM was organized on October 9, 1865. (Courtesy of Steve Davis.)

ILION MUNICIPAL BUILDING. The Ilion Municipal Building was opened in 1928 on the site of the old Morgan Street School. The last class graduated in 1913, and in 1927, the site was sold to the village. Before they moved to the new Morgan Street building, the village offices and police department were housed on Union Street, where they had a ready watch over all of the saloons on the street. (Courtesy of IL.)

ILION FIRE STATION. The Central Fire Station, located on Central Avenue in Ilion, was built in 1929. On December 15, 1929, it was opened to the public for inspection with a dinner held at the Hotel Osgood. To the left of the fire station is the Thompson Block, which dates back to the 1890s. On the right can be seen the side of the State Hotel. The hotel and the Thompson Block were razed for urban renewal. (Courtesy of IL.)

FIRE CHIEF'S CAR. Fire chief Sanford Getman (1899–1976), pictured in the car, and deputy chief Charles France (1905–1956), standing, show off Ilion's brand new Oldsmobile fire chief's car in October 1947. Sanford Getman was fire chief from 1922 until he retired in 1951. Charles France was appointed to succeed Getman as fire chief in 1952. (Courtesy of IL.)

Four

CHURCHES

EARLY VIEW OF ILION. This pleasant winter view looking towards Armory Hill was taken in 1865, when the construction of the Ilion Methodist Church was completed on the corner of West and Second Streets. To the left of the church can be seen a square brick house, which was owned by Nicolas Steele and torn down in 1924–1925. Towards the upper left is the Union Church, shortly after taken over by the Baptist Church. (Courtesy of IL.)

FORT HERKIMER CHURCH. The oldest church in Herkimer County and one of the oldest in New York State is the Fort Herkimer Church, located about 2 miles east of Mohawk. Built of native limestone, it was originally started in 1753 by Palatine German settlers but was only partially completed at the time of the French and Indian Wars. With the return of peace, construction resumed, and it was completed in 1767.

INTERIOR OF FORT HERKIMER CHURCH. The church was extensively rebuilt between 1812 and 1815; it was raised to a two-story height, an entrance and storm shelter were placed on the west end, and the original entrance was closed. Inside, a gallery was installed at the second-floor level, and the high pulpit was moved to the east side of the sanctuary. As the congregation began to shrink, even before the Civil War, the gallery was closed off and a ceiling installed beneath it to improve heating. Over the years, the congregation continued to diminish, and services gradually came to an end.

THANKSGIVING SERVICE. The Fort Herkimer Church was added to the State and National Registers of Historic Places in 1972 and is still used today for weddings and special events. Pictured is the 2009 Interfaith Service of Thanksgiving, which is held every year and organized by Don Fenner, chairman of the board of commissioners under the Montgomery Classis of the Reformed Church of America. The Thanksgiving service has been held since the 1930s, with several breaks during World War II and in the 1970s, when the church was undergoing renovation. Shown is the congregation, which is participating in a sing-along before the service. Robert Schmelcher, in the center aisle, helped accompany the sing-along on echo harp, while Paul Whitney, shown on the stairs at left, played the banjo. (Courtesy of Pamela Thompson.)

MOHAWK DUTCH REFORMED CHURCH. The congregation in Mohawk was formed at a meeting on December 11, 1838, when Christopher Bellinger and Samuel Meeker were elected elders and Samuel Barringer and Henry Harter deacons at the home of Maj. Frederick Bellinger. Their first church on Otsego Street was purchased from the Grace Episcopal Church. The pulpit was first occupied by Rev. James Murphy of Herkimer.

MODERN REFORMED CHURCH BUILT. The modern Reformed church on Otsego Street in Mohawk was built in 1962 after the previous church on the site was declared structurally unsafe and was demolished. The church is of A-frame type with a large front panel centered by a cross. The Sunday school wing was dedicated in June 1968. Shown is Mohawk mayor James Casey presenting an award to Rev. James Benes, pastor of the church. (Courtesy of Sharon Palmer.)

GRACE EPISCOPAL CHURCH. An Episcopal parish was organized in Mohawk in 1833. A church was built by Elias Root around 1837, but the congregation wasn't able to raise the funds for it and sold it to the Dutch Reformed church. It wasn't until 1887 that a new church was built and consecrated on East Main Street. In 1901, the brick residence adjacent to the church was purchased as a rectory through the efforts of Reverend Blacklock. (Courtesy of Jane Hyde.)

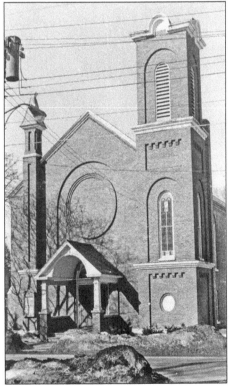

MOHAWK UNITED METHODIST CHURCH. The first Methodist congregation in Mohawk met in the old Columbia Street School from 1865 until four years later, when it was able to raise its own church building at 27 East Main Street under the leadership of Rev. Olin Wightman. It was incorporated in 1899. The church, as it is seen here, once had a much higher steeple that was torn down after it was struck by lightning in 1912.

INTERIOR OF METHODIST CHURCH. Shown in the late 1950s is the choir, directed by Blanche Rankins, during a Sunday morning service. From left to right are unidentified, Milford Miller, Mary Pond, Ruth Brown, Susan Harkins, unidentified, Bill Frankland, Bea Steffen, Alberta Reardon, and Lewis Innes. The organist, whose face is visible in the mirror, is Donald Reardon. (Courtesy of Mohawk Methodist Church.)

MOHAWK METHODIST SUNDAY SCHOOL. In 1956, an addition was completed to provide more rooms for Sunday school classes. Shown is teacher Vera Harwick conducting a class in the late 1950s. In 2001, the church congregation shared a minister with the parishes of Ilion and Frankfort. In the fall of 2007, the church council voted to close the Mohawk church and unite with Ilion and Frankfort. (Courtesy of Mohawk Methodist Church.)

BLESSED SACRAMENT ROMAN CATHOLIC CHURCH. In 1856, Mohawk was the first place to receive a resident pastor in this vicinity. Rev. William Howard took charge of the missions of Mohawk, Herkimer, Ilion, and Frankfort. Mass was celebrated in Varley's Hall until the Annunciation Church was built in Ilion in 1868. Years later, in 1901, Rev. John Quinn saw the need for a church in Mohawk and parishioner Mary Cronin purchased a lot to donate for its construction.

INTERIOR OF BLESSED SACRAMENT. The cornerstone was laid in October 1901, and the church was completed by the next year. It features memorial windows bearing the names of many of the early settlers of the Catholic faith. A house was purchased at the corner of Fulton and East Main Streets for a parochial residence. Shown is the 1946 wedding of Agnes Myers and Henry Thomes. (Courtesy of Agnes Thomes.)

NEW CHURCH BUILT. Replacement of the church was made necessary by structural deterioration leading to its demolition. Members worshipped in the parish hall from 1970 until September 1973, when a new Blessed Sacrament Church was built across the street. Shown is an interior shot of the new church during the 1983 wedding of Tom and Eileen Phalen. (Courtesy of Blessed Sacrament Church.)

MOHAWK UNIVERSALIST CHURCH. This small church in Mohawk on West Main Street near Grove Street was built after a Universalist congregation formed in Mohawk in 1850. The activities of the Mohawk Universalist Society closed with the termination of Rev. D. Ballou's ministry in 1878. It was later used by the Bible Baptist Church, a small autonomous Baptist denomination formed in the 1970s. Today it is the home of the Emmanuel Bible Church.

ILION UNITED METHODIST CHURCH.
Early Methodist worshippers met
in a common house of worship on
the site of the present First Baptist
Church. April 1860 found Ilion
becoming a Charge Church with the
Rev. D. B. White as pastor. A lot was
purchased at the corner of West and
Second Streets, and a cornerstone
for a new church was laid on
October 1, 1864. The building was
dedicated on January 3, 1866.

INTERIOR OF METHODIST CHURCH.
A signed Tiffany ascension window
was given in memory of Philo
and Caroline Remington in 1911.
In 1954, the church purchased
the Steele property between the
parsonage on Morgan Street and
the church, and construction of a
large wing for meetings and church
school was begun in 1958. Pictured
is Rev. Carlton Van Ornum (1955–
1966) with the choir. (Courtesy
of Ilion Methodist Church.)

ANNUNCIATION ROMAN CATHOLIC CHURCH. In 1867, a Catholic parish was established in Ilion, with Fr. William Howard leading the new congregation. Its towering steeple with a glittering gold cross beckoned parishioners until 1938, when a new church of Gothic design, seen here, was built on West Street and dedicated on March 27, 1938. The East Main Street church was purchased by Postmaster Thomas Morris, who with his sons, converted it into an auto sales and service agency.

SCHOOL OF THE ANNUNCIATION. On September 6, 1926, the doors of the new School of the Annunciation were opened to 170 pupils enrolled in the first four grades. It featured one of the largest auditoriums in the village of Ilion with a seating capacity of 800 and hosted many functions. The first graduating class was in June 1931. In 1961, the Convent for the Sisters of Mercy was completed on 61 West Street.

ANNUNCIATION CLASS OF 1933. From left to right are (first row) Norma Bubb, Frances Sullivan, Frances Grimm, Mary Gilmartin, Margaret Hopkins, Dorothy Donovan, Rev. James B. Gilloon, Helen Mendalka, Lucy Urtz, Agatha Hoeschele, Dorothy Polley, Dorothy Davis, and Genevieve Ward; (second row) John Chesebrough, William Carney, Howard Hoffman, James McGuiness, Theodore Bluett, Edward Hamilton, Raymond Lubey, Lawrence Brunette, James Paro, Edward Wachtman, Frances Yager, Joseph Pickett, Edward Snow, John McAllister, John Sweeney, John Parkinson, John Raux, John Beirne, Robert Hynes, Francis Murray, Philip Isom, and Albert Urtz. (Courtesy of Annunciation Church.)

ST. AUGUSTINE'S EPISCOPAL CHURCH. The church was founded on August 9, 1869, with Rev. Charles Lancaster as the first rector. The first church was in a building on Central Avenue. In 1913, a drive to raise funds for a new church was launched, and in 1915 a lot on Second Street was purchased. The rectory house at the front of the property was moved to the rear.

FIRST BAPTIST CHURCH. The Baptist congregation in Ilion was formed in 1865, with services held at the union worship center on Second Street. The congregation enlarged the church and dedicated it as a Baptist church in 1869. The building was demolished in 1896 and a new one built and dedicated on June 18, 1897. Pictured is the Ilion Baptist choir and orchestra in 1946. From left to right are (first row) M. Bump, unidentified, G. Bump, R. Heaps, and J. Schaepe; (second row) C. Paddock, R. Rowlands, D. Helmer, possibly W. Fitzer, M. Baker, S. Hendry, L. Bump, and C. Seiler; (third row) J. Harter, E. Lyman, A. Bennett, N. Wood, N. Waters, M. Rulus, M. Antoneros, M. Waters, J. Damon, D. Rathbun, L. Lyman, C. Deming, I. Hand, and F. Fay Swift; (fourth row) Reverend Ainslie, organist M. Windsor, unidentified, M. Lockyer, H. Paulus, M. Hayes, B. Hayes, V. Nelson, B. Bowdish, O. Coleman, M. Applegate, R. Harter, E. Kilbourne, E. Deming, B. Folmsbee, C. Wood, ? Bala, and unidentified. (Below courtesy of Ilion Baptist Church.)

FIRST PRESBYTERIAN CHURCH. The Presbyterian church in Ilion was organized on May 28, 1871, and first held its meetings in Mechanics Hall on First Street with Rev. D. M. Rankin as pastor. The congregation was able to purchase a lot on the corner of Morgan and Second Streets in 1874 to build its own church. On April 6, 1875, it saw its dream realized with the dedication of the new church building. The picture seen here is of the current church.

1912 FIRE. On February 11, 1912, shortly after Sunday school had been dismissed, smoke was discovered coming from the church. The fire quickly became a blazing inferno. The fire department responded promptly and contained it to the church, but all that remained were charred walls and the mammoth spire. While the fire was taking place, the church trustees were meeting across the street at the home of Dr. Richard Redway to discuss plans of rebuilding.

INTERIOR OF PRESBYTERIAN CHURCH. The cornerstone for the new church was laid on September 17, 1912. A new organ was purchased after the fire with the insurance settlement and a bequest of Mr. Frederick Weller of Mohawk. In 1943, the organ was rededicated as a result of several new additions and was one of the largest in the vicinity. Pictured is a communion service in 1940 with church elders. From left to right are F. D. Harter; Charles Miller; Thomas Suters; Dr. Paul Wagner, pastor; Wagner Kinaman; Kenneth Backus; Carl Flack; and Richard Dimock. (Courtesy of Ilion First Presbyterian Church.)

DENNISON CORNERS COMMUNITY CHURCH. This church, located on Route 28 south of Mohawk at the intersection of Vickerman Hill and Robinson Roads, was originally built in 1834 by Stanton Denison, a tavern owner from whom the hamlet derives its name. After being closed for a number of years, it was reopened in 1959 under the auspices of the American Mission for Opening Closed Churches and was rededicated in 1964. Today it is an active, independent, bible-centered church.

Five

SCHOOLS

FORT HERKIMER SCHOOL. Built in 1846, this one-room brick school is set on the west side of the Fort Herkimer Church. Pictured are students at the school around 1900. The teacher is Evington Sharpe of East Herkimer. Students are, from left to right, (first row) Laura Fisher, Wildora McCormick, Gus Lentz, Zadia Lightheart, Russel Bellinger, James Fox, unidentified, and Cleon Helmer; (second row) Zadia Harder, Gertrude Earl, May Helmer, Edna Bellinger, Della Eisenlord, ? Earl, Arthur Casler, Stanley McCormick, Frank Karasek, and Clyde Helmer. (Courtesy of Jack Morrison.)

MOHAWK'S FIRST SCHOOL. Mohawk's first schoolhouse was built in 1809 on the east side of Columbia Street just south of Michigan Street. It served for 44 years, until a new school was built in 1853 at Columbia and Washington Streets. Its usefulness continued, and it served as a meetinghouse for Methodists, a carpenter shop, and a waiting room for the Southern New York Railway before finally being torn down. (Courtesy of WL.)

THE SCHOOL THAT SPINNER BUILT. The school pictured here is the second one built at the intersection of Columbia Street and South Washington Street in Mohawk with room for all students in all the grades. Francis E. Spinner, with the support of his friends, formed a New School House Party and won the right to build the school. Known as the Mohawk Union School, it was eventually torn down to make way for the Columbia Street School. (Courtesy of WL.)

COLUMBIA STREET SCHOOL. In 1892–1893, the new three-story brick Columbia Street School was built on the site of the old one. The first through eighth grades were on the first floor, the high school students were on the second floor, and a science room and a museum were on the third floor. It was torn down after 1957 to make way for the new municipal building. (Courtesy of Lil Gaherty.)

SECOND GRADE, COLUMBIA STREET SCHOOL. This picture is of the second grade class in front of Columbia Street School in 1918. Pictured from left to right are (first row) Ethel Hopkins, Ersula Coffin, Nella Joslin, Arline Crim, Mildred Firman, unidentified, Ward Fenton, unidentified, J. Eugene Jackson, unidentified, Theron Hurdic, and Frederick Aherne; (second row) ? Aherne, unidentified, Stanley Hoke, Olga Cary, Regina Harris, two unidentified, Lynn Fenton, two unidentified, and Robert Gokey; (third row) unidentified, Stuart Chrisman, ? Brown, Omer Geesler, unidentified, Sam Keller, Veronica Haran, Charles Drury, two unidentified, Mildred Edwards, and two unidentified. (Courtesy of Marilyn Bridger.)

GRADE SCHOOL CHILDREN. This c. 1921–1922 photograph shows a grade at the Columbia Street School. Those who are identified are Lucille Burton and Loretta Acquilar (Adams), sixth and seventh from the left in the second row; Rita Geesler and Ida Jane Hammond (Quackenbush), first and second from the right in the second row, and possibly Richard Brown at the far right in the front row (Courtesy of Ron Keno.)

MOHAWK HIGH SCHOOL. In 1915, a lot was purchased on Grove Street and a school was built to house the high school students. In 1929 and again in 1950, additions were made, making room for a gym, 28 more classrooms, a shop room, agriculture and homemaking facilities, and a large auditorium seating 800. The school was renamed the Gregory B. Jarvis School in memory of the Mohawk native who was killed on the space shuttle *Challenger* in 1986.

1925 GRADUATING CLASS OF MOHAWK. Pictured are, from left to right, (first row) Ruth Shumway, Ida ?, Molly Wagner, Elizabeth Darvaux, Elsie Schmidt, Doris Gorham, Blanche Woodford, Almira Schaufler, Anna Carpenter, and Ruth Brown; (second row) Ray Callman, Richard Clark, Francis Ahern, Lorraine Failing, William Farnell, David Rix, Warren Ranney, James Graves, Lynn Wright, Tilden Arthur, and Lawrence Paul. (Courtesy of Lawrence Clark.)

1928 GRADUATING CLASS OF MOHAWK. Pictured are, from left to right, (first row) Margaret Lahey, Sidney Robertson, Helen Watson, Nelson Burton, Catherine Moore, Richard Gerstenberg, Ethel Teschmacher, Carroll Hassett, Eunice Shannon, and Marion Hinman; (second row) Rosemary Millar, George Thomes Jr., unidentified, James Coffin, Pearl Loopman, Marjorie Streitz, John Cook, Marie Brown, James Hanlon, and Evelyn Edgett; (third row) Dorlon Pond, James Robbins, Harold Edick, Samuel Dennison, Robert Rankins, and Ralph Thomes.

1931 GRADUATING CLASS OF MOHAWK. Pictured are, from left to right, (first row) possibly Marian Griswold, Mary Moynihan, unidentified, Paul Townsend, Helen Gerstenberg, Clifford Judd, Evelyn Owens, Edgar Hicks, unidentified, Virginia Quackenbush, and unidentified; (second row) Grover Shoemaker, unidentified, Eddie Walsh, Dallas Pearl Petrie, Marion Brazie, Helen Harris, two unidentified, James Bleaking, Robert Knapp, and unidentified; (third row) Fred Ludwig, unidentified, Donald Smith, Howard Thomes, two unidentified, and Lawrence Dibble. Listed with the picture but not identified are Lewis Innes, Eunice Edwards, Gertrude Haran, Howard Newman, Gordon Smith, and Ann Virginia Tompkins. (Courtesy of Pamela Shoemaker.)

MOHAWK SCHOOL BASKETBALL TEAM OF 1926–1927. From left to right are (seated) Dayton Delong, Carrol Hassett, Jack Cook, James Robbins, and James Hanlon; (standing) Coach Ahrens, Richard Gerstenberg, Robert Knapp, James Cook, and manager Lawrence Clark. (Courtesy of Lawrence Clark.)

MOHAWK SCHOOL BASKETBALL TEAM OF **1928–1929.** From left to right are (first row) Taylor Harter, Bernard Ryan, and Eddie O'Connor; (second row) ? Shoemaker, Gordon Townsend, ? Munn, ? Louis, and Ward Fenton; (third row) physical training teacher Harold Hausner and the captain, who is unidentified. (Courtesy of Marilyn Bridger.)

MOHAWK GIRLS SPORTS TEAM. Pictured is a girls' sports team from Mohawk around 1934. From left to right are (first row) Katherine Lynch Miles, ? Rankins, Marion Armstrong Partington, Marguerite Crouse, Harriet Warren Busher, and Sylvia Miller; (second row) Eleanor Bergin Helmer, Bernice Bergin Hennessey, Rita Cavannaugh, Arlene Hilts Crogan, and Dorothy Harter Wilkins; (third row) unidentified, Clara Rankins, Susan Innes, Roberta Hammond, and coach Emily Hall Lynch. (Courtesy of Ron Keno.)

MOHAWK HIGH CHAMPS. The Mohawk girls basketball team of 1934–1935 is, from left to right, Dorothy Harter, forward; Marguerite Crouse, center forward; Harriet Warren, guard center; Sylvia Miller, guard; Eleanor Bergen, guard; Rita Cavanaugh, guard; Susan Innes, guard; Arlene Hilts, forward; Herberta Hammond, forward; and Catherine Lynch, forward and team captain. (Courtesy of Ron Keno.)

MOHAWK SCHOOL FOOTBALL TEAM. Shown are members of the 1937 "Mighty Midgets" football team, who were honored at a testimonial dinner for winning the county championship. From left to right are (first row) Jamon Barnum, Pete Corey, Francis O'Connor, Herbert Marmet, Arthur Hausner, Stanley Fistick, Michael Holowaty, and Robert Ray; (second row) manager Doug Monroe, Glen Danforth, Francis Lynch, William Busher, Henry Thomes, and coach William Fenner. (Courtesy of Jane Hyde.)

MOHAWK DRUM CORPS. Pictured is the Mohawk Drum Corps in 1944 at the Mohawk Village Hall. Standing in the middle is Audry Sponburg, and forming a "V" around her are, from left to right, Doris Spencer, Helen Hammond, unidentified, Betty Johnson, Bev Beniduk, Dot LaVenture, Alice Smallenberger, and Joan Bellinger. (Courtesy of Alice Haefele.)

FIRE AT MOHAWK CENTRAL SCHOOL. On October 21, 1994, residents woke up to discover the Jarvis High School in Mohawk was in flames. The Mohawk Fire Department worked tirelessly to battle the blaze, assisted by fire departments from Ilion, Frankfort, Herkimer, East Herkimer, and Cedarville. The fire consumed the library, chemistry lab, offices, and two dozen classrooms.

MORGAN STREET SCHOOL. The Morgan Street School was built in 1865 as a three-story addition to an earlier stone school building on 41–51 Morgan Street in Ilion. It was built on the expansive front lawn facing Morgan Street. Another addition was built in 1884, and the school continued to operate, graduating its last class in 1913. (Courtesy of IL.)

ARBOR DAY AT MORGAN STREET SCHOOL. This 1897 photograph shows students planting trees in front of the school in honor of Arbor Day. Pictured from left to right are Edward Baker, Arnon Comstock, Frank Jenne, Maude Gay, Lena Keller, William Wilfert, Emma White, Leroy Shineman, Etta Cox, principal Judson I. Wood, Wheatley Tisdale, Catherine Nunn, H. H. Halliwell, Jennie Heiland, George Edick, Carrie Jockmus, Thomas Carney, Maude Birch, Lucius Robson, and C. Joseph Diss. (Courtesy of IL.)

1904 GRADUATING CLASS. Thirteen of the 16 members of the 1904 graduating class at the Morgan Street School posed for this picture. The class consisted of Earl Avery, Harris Beebe, Edith Bell, Bessie Cone, Erma Crim, Mabel Daly, Mae Devendorf, Charles Gordon, Marion Hakes, Jessie Hartford, Ina Hubbard, Czarina Lobdell, John Maury, Ethel Penny, Anna Reilly, and David Springer. (Courtesy of IL.)

WEST HILL SCHOOL. To ease the overcrowding of the Morgan Street School, land was purchased on Second Street in Ilion in 1896 to build a new school for the youth of that area. On April 30, 1897, the six-room brick building was dedicated and called the West Hill School. This picture was taken in 1910. The school was enlarged to 14 rooms with a gymnasium in 1925. After the school closed, the Marine Corps League took over the use of the building. (Courtesy of IL.)

Second Grade Class, 1964–1965. Pictured is the West Hill Elementary School second grade class of 1964–1965 with teacher Diane Sterzin. Shown from left to right are (first row) Cissy Hoffman, unidentified, Tom Streeter, Bob McDowell, and Mary Hartman; (second row) unidentified, David Irving, unidentified, Mary Beachard, and unidentified; (third row) Mark Williams, Scott Holden, Jim Trevett, Ann Marie Murphy, and Daryl Burke; (fourth row) Nancy Stubley, unidentified, Joel Layaw, Debbie Doolen, and Lisa Albin. (Courtesy of IL.)

North Street School. North Street School was built with six rooms in 1906 at 39 East North Street in Ilion. It was enlarged to 14 rooms in 1916, and a third story was added in 1927 for a gymnasium and auditorium. In 1951, a new gymnasium and cafeteria were added. The principal from 1923 to 1952 was Ethel Campbell, who retired in 1958. (Courtesy of Tim Daly.)

THIRD GRADE CLASS, 1944–1945. Pictured is Viva Spink's third-grade class from September 1944 to June 1945. The picture was taken in April 1945. The North Street School closed in 1977 and was given to the Full Gospel Church for their use with Michael Servello as pastor. Today it is an apartment building. (Courtesy of Pat Couchman.)

ILION HIGH SCHOOL. Ilion High School, at 99 Weber Avenue, was built in 1914 and enlarged by two wings in 1925 and by a gymnasium in 1927. The athletic field and tennis court in back of the school were obtained from the Ilion Cemetery Association in 1933. In 1951, ten rooms were added, including a music room and cafeteria, and the back stage was remodeled.

ILION HIGH BASKETBALL TEAM, 1918–1919. Pictured from left to right are (first row) unidentified, ? Rasbach, and Tommy Scott; (second row) Charles Punk Jones, Kenneth Yeomans, Kenneth O'Neil, and Charles Mallery. (Courtesy of IL.)

ILION HIGH SCHOOL FIRE. A deadly fire on April 22, 1963, ripped through Ilion's Junior-Senior High School on Weber Avenue and cost the life of fireman Burton Seymour. The blaze started on the third floor of the original high school building, which was constructed in 1914. Some 25 classrooms were destroyed or damaged as well as the school auditorium, the girls' gymnasium, administrative offices, and the new language laboratory. (Courtesy of IL.)

Six

BUSINESS AND INDUSTRY

FOUNDRY OF CHAUNCEY JOHNSON. Pictured is the foundry of Chauncey Johnson (1811–1876) at the end of Warren Street in Mohawk, on the bank of the Erie Canal, around 1870. Many of the iron fences in front of the homes in Mohawk, as well as fancy urns, fountains, and ballasters, were made there. While attending the Emancipation Day parade in Washington, Johnson invited a freed black couple to live in Mohawk. Anthony and Mary Miller took him up on that offer and worked for the Johnsons; they are buried in Mohawk cemetery. (Courtesy of WL.)

MOHAWK MILLING AND MALTING COMPANY. This short-lived company began in 1894 on the Erie Canal near the West Shore depot as one entered Mohawk from Herkimer. The company bought, sold, and ground grain, flour, and feed and also carried on a malting business. Its manager, Charles Young (1856–1923), operated the mill until 1906, when it became a table factory called the Mohawk Manufacturing Company. The building burned in 1907. (Courtesy of WL.)

MOHAWK VALLEY BANK. Banking in Mohawk has been conducted in this building on the corner of West Main and Washington Streets for more than a century. Mohawk's first bank, the National Mohawk Valley Bank, founded in 1839, became the National Bank of Mohawk in 1865. It closed in 1931 during the Great Depression but reopened in 1940 as a branch of Oneida National Bank and Trust Company. It is now part of Adirondack Bank. (Courtesy of Lil Gaherty.)

MORGAN EDWARDS LUNCH WAGON. Morgan Edwards' lunch wagon stood at the corner of Otsego and Main Streets from 1907 to about 1920. The lunch wagon is typical of the time when villages turned to electrically powered cars rather than horse-drawn trolleys. The old cars were sold, and many ended up as lunch wagons. They were popular because workers and pedestrians could purchase inexpensive meals. In the background is Flanders General Store. (Courtesy of Marilyn Bridger.)

DEVENDORF DRY GOODS STORE. Ralph Devendorf and his wife, Florence, operated a grocery and dry goods business on the north side of Main Street in Mohawk during the 1880s. In the 1890s, they dropped the groceries and advertised their business as "dry goods, crockery and wallpaper." This photograph appears to be from the 1890s; note the crockery in the window on the left. (Courtesy of WL.)

MARTIN AUTOMATIC FISH REEL COMPANY. The company was started in Ilion in the 1880s, when Herman Martin developed a reel that would enable fishermen to control their slack lines and prevent tangles. He partnered with Remington to start his company and started in the Novelty Works building. In 1901, the building was sold and moved to Mohawk. It manufactured its own reel product line until it closed its doors in 1992. (Courtesy of Jane Hyde.)

"Mart" with his "Martin" in action at a critical moment
MARTIN AUTOMATIC FISH REEL CO., ILION, N.Y.

MOHAWK VALLEY HOTEL. The Mohawk Valley Hotel was located on the northwest corner of Main and Otsego Streets in Mohawk. Built in 1874, it contained 50 guest rooms, a dining room, and an opera house, as well as space for offices and seven stores. The hotel burned March 16, 1900. The records in the town clerk's office, located in the building, were destroyed, as were the charter and furnishings for the Masonic lodge. (Courtesy of WL.)

AFTER THE HOTEL. This later picture shows the same location on the northwest corner of Main and Otsego Streets in Mohawk after the fire. The property was sold in 1902 to Charles Bates, who constructed a new hotel to replace the Mohawk Valley Hotel. The building, pictured here with bay windows, was also destroyed by fire in 1966. (Courtesy of WL.)

BATES THEATER. Built in 1843 by Hendrick Lodge of the International Order of Odd Fellows, Odd Fellows Hall had a 1,000-seat auditorium and was the only opera house in the vicinity. In 1875, the building was purchased by the Mohawk Valley Hotel and used as a livery stable. Following the hotel's destruction by fire in 1900, the building was remodeled and opened as Bates Theater in 1914. Later used as a skating rink, it finally closed and was razed in 1935.

MOHAWK HOUSE. One of Mohawk's most well known hotels was the Mohawk House, built in 1835 on the corner of Columbia and East Main Streets. One of its first proprietors was Allan Bennett, followed by Abelard May, J. Casler, and Albert Pickart. First John and then his brother Seth Mabbett operated it in the late 1800s. The hostelry was razed in 1942. (Courtesy of Jane Hyde.)

RICHARDSON HARDWARE COMPANY. The gentlemen of the Mohawk Club prepare for an outing in June 1913. The men have their vehicles displayed in front of Richardson's Hardware Store at the corner of Main and Warren Streets in Mohawk. Jacob Richardson started the store in the 1880s and handed it down to his son Burton, who operated it until the early 1920s. The next proprietor, Harold Ray, ran the Mohawk Hardware Company for many years. (Courtesy of Ron Keno.)

PARAGON KNITTING MILL. This building has a long history as a knitting mill on East Main Street in Mohawk. It was first the Knitting Company of Mohawk in 1890 but became the Paragon Knitting Mill in 1895, as pictured here. It was sold in 1909 to the Muldoon Underwear Company, manufacturing hygienic underwear designed by the famous Dr. Muldoon, who treated patients for nervous ailments. The company was sold in 1913 to the Elastic Spring Knit Corporation. (Courtesy of Lil Gaherty.)

ELASTIC SPRING KNIT CORPORATION. This shot shows workers at the Elastic Spring Knit Corporation. Mabel Eckhart is seen in front, third from the right, and Nan Crogan is standing in the back at the far right. When it was in full operation, more than 200 hands were employed manufacturing a full line of wool ribbed underwear in men's, women's and children's union suits. In 1929, it was purchased by McLaughlin-Stevens, manufacturers of library equipment. (Courtesy of Thelma Miles.)

KNITTING MILL NOW A FACTORY OUTLET. McLaughlin-Stevens operated until the late 1930s. In 1943, Louis and Morton Kowalsky purchased the plant for a warehouse but sold it to the Paper Drapery Corporation by 1947. In 1956, Mohawk merchant Thomas Fahy purchased it and operated the Mohawk Mill Bargain Center, pictured here, until the mid-1960s. Today it is the factory Outlet Depot and Herkimer County Community College student housing.

DUOFOLD IN MOHAWK. Duofold manufactured special knit underwear that became famous all over the country and still is today. In 1977, it moved its knitting operation to the Sperry Univac building in Ilion. In 1986, the Scottish firm Dawson International purchased Duofold and moved its operations to Pennsylvania with manufacturing still in Ilion, which was shut down in 1998. The Mohawk building burned on June 9, 2000. (Courtesy of Jane Hyde.)

SUNOCO SERVICE STATION. Glenn Lyons operated this Sunoco service station at the corner of Main and Columbia Streets in Mohawk from 1947 to 1952. It is on the site of the former Mohawk House hotel. Charles Comstock then operated it as a Gulf station until 1980. The business, now known as Lawrence Paul's, continues to serve the village residents. (Courtesy of Sharon Clapper.)

KWIK-KUT MANUFACTURING. One of Mohawk's lasting businesses, Kwik-Kut Manufacturing moved from Ilion to Columbia Street in Mohawk in 1955. John Fitzer bought the business from William Carter in 1968 and added more products, such as Deluxe Choppers, Egg Fry Rings, and Koffee Koolers. In 1989, Fitzer's daughter Mary Morse bought the company and operates the business today. (Courtesy of Mary Morse.)

ATLANTIC AND PACIFIC TEA COMPANY. The Mohawk High School Marching Band parades down Main Street in Mohawk around 1940. The Great Atlantic and Pacific Tea Company (A&P) store in the background was located at 32 West Main Street. The A&P was the first national supermarket chain in the United States. (Courtesy of Rosemary Williams Brown.)

OLD REMINGTON FORGE. The story of how Ilion grew to be an important manufacturing metropolis starts with a young man who wanted a gun. In 1816, Eliphalet Remington Jr., using his father's forge and scrap iron, fashioned a gun barrel and took it to a gunsmith in Utica for rifling. The Utica gunsmith was impressed with Eliphalet's creation and told potential gun buyers. The demand led to the beginnings of a small business.

FIRST REMINGTON FACTORY. The opening of the Erie Canal in 1825 made it easier to ship the guns to a wider market. Eliphalet would walk the 4 miles to the canal bridge, a board was lifted from the floor, and the package was dropped onto a passing boat. By 1828, Eliphalet bought property in Ilion, the Old Armory was built, and the Remington Arms Company had begun. (Courtesy of IL.)

THE OLD ARMORY. Philo Remington joined the firm in 1837, followed by Samuel in 1839 and Eliphalet III 10 years later. Each son brought a special talent to the company. The first government contract was awarded to the Remington firm in 1845, when war was looming with Mexico. (Courtesy of Tim Daly.)

E. REMINGTON AND SONS. The Remingtons branched out into other products. By the 1870s, they were manufacturing agricultural implements, sewing machines, an electric light system, and typewriters. The Remington interest in other patents and inventions remained strong. Unfortunately, economic cycles led the Remingtons to become overextended, and in February 1888, E. Remington and Sons was sold to the firm of Hartley and Graham. In the background, the Remington Mansion can be seen. (Courtesy of IL.)

REMINGTON ARMS COMPANY. Harley and Graham, which also owned Union Metallic Cartridge Company, adopted contemporary management techniques, changed the name to Remington Arms Company, and introduced bicycles, farm equipment, and other goods into the company's product line. The tide began to turn and the firm was in recovery. It has seen ups and downs, but it continues to this day and is a mainstay in the Ilion community. (Courtesy of Remington Arms.)

REMINGTON TYPEWRITER WORKS. The Remington Typewriter Works was originally owned by the Remingtons but was sold in 1886 to Wycoff, Seamans, and Benedict (William Wycoff, Clarence Walker Seamans, and Henry Harper Benedict). The new owners opened sales offices and typing schools abroad and expanded until they ran out of capacity. The building pictured here was built in 1898, and by 1902 the Ilion factories had 1,500 employees who produced 50,000 machines a year. (Courtesy of Tim Daly.)

A STRIKE IN 1936. The typewriter company was the scene of a historic strike in 1936 when its officers refused to allow their workers to join the American Federation of Labor (AFL). It took AFL leadership, U.S. secretary of labor Frances Perkins, and company president James Rand Jr. to work out a settlement. (Courtesy of Nancy Cioch.)

TYPEWRITER MONUMENT. A view looking from Catherine Street shows the typewriter monument near the front of the Remington factory building with the waters of the old canal behind it. To the right of the canal can be seen railroad tracks. These were the spur tracks from the West Shore Railroad that led to the Remington typewriter factories. (Courtesy of Mark Eddy.)

RETIREMENT PARTY. A group of Remington employees from the electric department gathered for a retirement party for Fred Egger at the Black and White restaurant in the Ilion Gorge in 1949. Pictured clockwise from left are John Ropenski, Harold Voorhees, Harold Macon, Paul Cambridge, Vern Eddy, Alan Lake, Ken Robinson, Fred Egger, George Friis, Ben Mills, Nick Carter, Alton Pickert, Ernest Primmar, John Steele, and Earl McLain. (Courtesy of Paul Cambridge.)

REMINGTON SOCIETY OF AMERICA. In 1982, a group of collectors formed the Remington Society of America (RSA) to further the study of antique Remington firearms. Each year, an RSA team visits Ilion to conduct research. Pictured is the RSA team in 1994 with Jane Spellman (seated) and, from left to right, Leon Wier Jr., Jay Huber, Roy Marcot, Kevin Cornell, Slim Kohler, and Jerry Swinney. (Courtesy of Remington Arms.)

ILION'S FIRST BUSINESS BLOCK. Ilion's first business block, on Main Street near Otsego Street, is pictured in 1870. The block is shown first on an 1857 map and lists J. M. Dygert as a grocer, Merry and Devoe shippers, Grimes and Lewis hardware, and a boot and shoe store. By 1870, the businesses housed in this block included George and Harry Wilcox Fine Clothing (left) and Reuben Hotaling Groceries and Liquors (right). (Courtesy of IL.)

UNION STREET. An early shot of Union Street in Ilion taken in 1884 shows the street looking south from Main Street. Union Street was between Otsego and Morgan Streets and does not exist today, being covered over by urban renewal in the early 1970s. (Courtesy of Joe Putnam.)

THE TEN COMMANDMENTS. Every community seemed to have one, and Ilion's Ten Commandment buildings were on Union Street. The name comes from the 10 businesses that existed in the block, which included at that time five saloons, a tailor, a bottling works, a Chinese laundry, and an unidentified business. This shot appears to have been taken right after a huge fire ripped through the area in 1890. (Courtesy of IL.)

THE OLD BREWERY. A brewery sat at the end of West Canal Street on the Erie Canal since 1859, when James Dygert operated it. Sayer Spedding, of England, took over the brewery in the 1870s, and James Mooney operated it in the 1890s until the company went bankrupt in 1897. The community around the brewery was known as "Skimmerville" because many residents worked at the brewery. (Courtesy of IL.)

D. C. FOLEY BLACKSMITH SHOP. Daniel Foley (1847–1907) purchased the Riddell Blacksmith shop at 44 West Main Street in Ilion and conducted his shop in the village for many years. He served his country in the Civil War in the 121st Regiment and was wounded at Spotsylvania. Identified in the picture, in the center, is Bob Foley, Daniel's son. (Courtesy of IL.)

O. B. RUDD JEWELRY STORE. Pictured is the Rudd Jewelry Store at the corner of Main and Otsego Streets in Ilion some time before 1890. The business was established in 1862 by Orange B. Rudd, who also owned the rest of the building. It later was known as Rudd and Rix when Walter Rix became a partner in the firm in 1907. (Courtesy of IL.)

GETMAN GROCERY STORE. Fayette Getman and Sons Grocery was established in 1901 on the corner of Otsego and Main Streets in Ilion. Fayette Getman (1847–1919), pictured second from the left, operated the store with his two sons, Clarence (1883–1947) and George (1879–1954). The grocery store moved to 28 Otsego Street some time after Fayette's death. (Courtesy of IL.)

CHANDLER'S GROCERY. Herbert Chandler (1868–1934) ran a grocery store in the village of Ilion for 28 years, first at 31 First Street in the early 1900s. By 1913, he moved his grocery to 7 West Main Street, pictured here. By 1921, his son Roy Chandler went into partnership with him, and the store was named H. B. Chandler and Son. In 1929, the store was sold to the A&P. (Courtesy of IL.)

OSGOOD HOTEL. The Osgood Hotel was built in 1852 on the corner of Otsego and Main Streets in Ilion by Eliphalet Remington. It was later known as the Briggs Hotel and Hotel Gammond until 1894, when it was again known as the Osgood House. In 1992, a part of the building was demolished for the Manufacturers National Bank, and the remaining structure was razed in the 1970s during urban renewal. (Courtesy of IL.)

CLARKE AND BAKER COMPANY. This convoy of cars, pictured outside the New Osgood Hotel, was shuttling dignitaries to various events surrounding the grand opening of the new factory of the Clarke and Baker Company in 1906. They were soon acquired by the Library Bureau, which retained its name until 1909 and later moved to Harkimer. (Courtesy of Remington Arms.)

ILION GORGE HOTEL. Built in 1849, the United States Hotel on the Ilion Gorge Road was a popular attraction for nearly 75 years because of its scenic location and access to sulfur water. In 1915, it was remodeled and renamed the Ilion Gorge Hotel, boasting running water in every room, as well as sulfur water piped to rooms especially fitted for sulfur bath treatments. The hotel was torn down in 1921. (Courtesy of IL.)

MANSION HOUSE. The Mansion House hotel stood at the corner of Central Avenue and East Clark Street and was reputed to be one of the leading hotels of Ilion. The hotel was purchased in 1893 by Patrick Flahaven, who enlarged it with a three-story addition and operated it until his death in 1928. The building was razed in 1933. (Courtesy of IL.)

COMMERCIAL HOTEL. This hotel, at 34 Otsego Street in Ilion, has been a longtime fixture known in later years as Harter's Beach. Thomas Mitchell was an early proprietor who first gave it the name Commercial Hotel. Mitchell's housekeeper, Louisa Schmidt, would later run it with her husband, Henry Halpin, as the Otsego House. After Louisa's death, her husband and her daughter Anna and Anna's husband, Harry Harter, ran the hotel. The building was razed in 1980. (Courtesy of IL.)

STATE HOTEL. First known as the Old Homestead when it had its grand opening on December 12, 1910, at 7 Canal Street in Ilion, it soon became known as Remmer's Hotel after its owner Frederick Remmer. Some time between 1929 and 1936, it changed its name to Copernoll's Hotel after proprietor Robert Copernoll, and around 1948, it became the State Hotel, run by Lena Rieck until her death in 1964. Merle and Marion Saunders were its last proprietors when it was razed druing urban renewal. (Courtesy of IL.)

L. L. MERRY STORE. At the corner of East Main and Otsego Streets in Ilion, Lawrence Ludlow Merry operated a grocery and provision store from 1869 to 1876. Prior to this, he had been a member of the assembly in 1847 and served as postmaster from 1860 to 1864. The Remington factory, seen up the street, was erected in 1861, when the Remington family decided to manufacture guns on a large scale. (Courtesy of Remington Arms.)

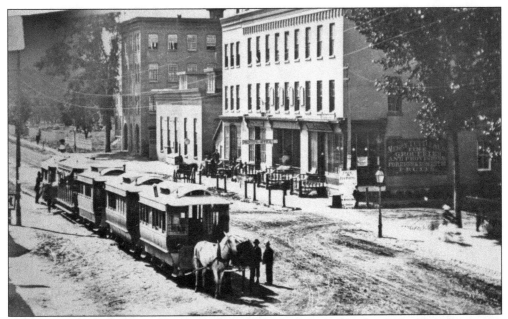

MERRY AND TUTTLE. The block on East Main and Otsego Streets in the 1880s shows the grocery store on the corner, now operated by L. L. Merry's son Seward Merry under Merry and Tuttle. He was also an agent for the American Express Company at that place. Next-door is the printing office of the *Ilion Citizen*, and further down is the Remington Armory building. (Courtesy of Remington Arms.)

THE BANK BLOCK. This early-1920s picture shows the 4–8 East Main Street block in Ilion, known as the Bank Block because two banks were located here—Ilion National Bank (formed in 1867 to succeed the Ilion Bank, founded 15 years earlier by Eliphalet II) and the Ilion Loan Association. Also located here were the Ilion Chamber of Commerce, Reed's Clothing Store, and the Rudd and Rix jewelry store, operated by J. Holland Rudd and Walter Rix. The block lives on as the last remnant of East Main Street. (Courtesy of Remington Arms.)

LONGTIME PHARMACY IN ILION. This building on the corner of Central Avenue and West Canal Street housed a drugstore from the 1880s up to 1955. The first owner, Dr. Eugene Draper, sold it to his drug clerk, Sarah Carney, when he moved to California in 1902. When Sarah married in 1906, she turned the business over to her younger brother, George Carney. Samuel Swann operated it in the 1930s, and Robert Mulvey was the last owner in 1955, when he moved his business to Otsego Street. (Courtesy of IL.)

CAPITOL THEATER. Owners Frank Whitney and Ben Young built the Capitol Theater in 1925 and added the business block along Otsego Street in 1927. The theater, with a seating capacity of 1,200, also boasted a ballroom and bowling alleys. The theater eventually became part of the Schine theater chain and closed in 1966. This photograph was taken in 1969. (Courtesy of IL.)

FIRST STREET, 1962. The view down Ilion's First Street frames the Odd Fellows temple on the corner of Morgan Street. The Odd Fellows first organized in 1874 and met in several places before constructing this imposing building about 1905. It boasted a theater on the upper floors in addition to the group's lodge rooms. The theater was open to the public but declined in popularity after the Capitol Theater was built in 1925. (Courtesy of IL.)

THE BEST GARAGE. From its beginning in 1924, the Best Garage at 48 West Main Street in Ilion always lived up to its motto, "We Never Close." In an era when most businesses closed by 9:00 p.m. and didn't open on Sundays, the Best Garage, owned by Alex Reardon, stayed open to serve the area's motorists 24 hours a day. It finally closed in the late 1960s and was razed during urban renewal. (Courtesy of IL.)

MICKEY'S DINER. Mickey's Diner, at 44 West Main Street near Best Furniture and the A&P Store, was an Ilion landmark before urban renewal dramatically changed the downtown area. The dining car–style diner was opened by Frank (Mickey) Bentz in the late 1930s, and though owned by several different people over the years, it retained its original name until closing in the late 1960s. (Courtesy of IL.)

MOORE'S NEWSSTAND. This building at 23 Central Avenue was a newsstand for many years serving the residents of Ilion. It was first owned by William Staley, who ran a confectionery before he turned it into a newsstand in the 1930s. Some time between 1949 and 1951, Merle Moore and his wife, Mildred, took the shop over under the name of Moore's Newsstand. (Courtesy of IL.)

FLATIRON BUILDING. This flatiron-shaped building at the corner of Otsego and West Streets in Ilion was built in 1914. It has served as the Panarites grocery and confectionery store, Gold and Brown Restaurant, Corner Snacks shop, Hendrick Crossway Corner Store, Pizza Point, Pizza Works, The Hangar, and now Flat Iron Pizza. This picture was taken on February 18, 1962. (Courtesy of IL.)

DOTY'S FARM. This picture shows strawberry pickers at Doty's farm in the early 1900s. The patch was located on Barringer Road on the outskirts of Ilion. Abner Doty and his son cultivated 25 acres in 1862. In 1886, Ilion growers organized into the Ilion Strawberry Association and Fruit Growers' Exchange with offices in downtown stores. The farm was later a dairy, but today the field in this picture is the ninth fairway of Doty's Golf Course. (Courtesy of IL.)

ILION HOSPITAL. The hospital was incorporated in 1906 under the name of Ilion Emergency Hospital, and the cornerstone was laid in 1908 on a hill above West Main Street (today Sixth Avenue). It was formally opened on June 19, 1909, and renamed the Henry Harper Benedict Hospital after a major donor. At his request, the name was changed to Ilion Hospital. Dr. Jennie Richardson, who was active in the establishment of the hospital, served as president of the Women's Associate Hospital Board for 39 years and was made honorary president of the group in 1948. Plans were made for a bigger hospital in 1962, and it was called the Mohawk Valley General Hospital. In 1972, a nursing home was built adjacent and connected to the hospital. Today it operates solely as a nursing home. (Courtesy of Nelson Pardee.)

Seven

TRANSPORTATION

FORT HERKIMER ROAD. The dirt roadway seen in this picture is the Fort Herkimer Road, today known as Route 5S. A corner of the Fort Herkimer Church can be seen on the far right and the Fort Herkimer School on the extreme left. The one-room school, built in 1846, had double desks and was heated by a woodstove. In the background can be seen the newly developed East Herkimer, which received more residents after the 1910 Herkimer flood.

THE TROLLEY IN MOHAWK. A Herkimer, Mohawk, Ilion, and Frankfort electric trolley sits in front of the Mohawk Valley Hotel. The trolley business was in operation in 1870, when it was only 1.75 miles long and was horse-drawn. By 1872, it was electrified, and by 1902, it connected with Utica. Eventually known as the New York State Electric Railway, the valley trolley was 37 miles long, double-tracked, and provided service every half hour. (Courtesy of Lil Gaherty.)

THE RIOT IN MOHAWK. In 1904, when the Oneonta, Cooperstown, and Richfield Springs Railroad (OC&RS) wanted to connect its line on Columbia Street with that of the Utica and Mohawk Valley Electric Railroad on Main Street, the village asked for $15,000. The OC&RS refused and continued work. A crowd gathered, and fire hoses were sprayed on the Italian laborers, stopping work that day. The work was completed the next day under a guard of deputies. This photograph was taken around 1910. (Courtesy of Lynn Roof.)

TROLLEY ACCIDENT IN ILION. The electric trolley car of the Herkimer–Frankfort line derailed in front of 273 West Main Street in Ilion on July 2, 1920. The car dropped part of its motor or brake construction on the track near the London Bridge in Ilion, derailing the car. Fortunately, the rear tracks of the car caught on the bank, preventing it from plunging into the canal.

CANAL PACKET BOAT *D. D. WINSTON*. The steam packet boat D. D. Winston can be seen docked on the Erie Canal near West Main Street in Ilion with a load of passengers ready to go on an excursion. It was captained by Andrew J. Budlong. In 1894, the *D. D. Winston* collided with another boat and sank near Utica. While no one was hurt, the boat was a total loss. (Courtesy of IL.)

BARGE CANAL LOCK 18. Improvement on the old Erie Canal waterway, widening and dredging its channels to make way for bigger boats, led to the construction of the Barge Canal in 1903. It was officially completed on May 15, 1918. Work on Lock 18 at Jacksonburg was started in 1910. Work on the canal from Jacksonburg to Herkimer was completed in 1916. In 1985, the New York State Department of Transportation purchased the 2-mile-long Plantation Island in the Mohawk River near the lock. The island was transferred to the New York State Department of Environmental Conservation (DEC) for use as a wildlife preserve. Boaters, locally and from around the world, travel through the lock's gates and enjoy the area's natural scenery. Shown is the building of Lock 18. Arthur Casler ran the derrick. The second photograph is of the completed lock. (Above courtesy of Ann Casler Green.)

GROCERY STORE ON THE OLD ERIE CANAL. Hawley (1850–1913) and Ella (1861–1951) Casler operated a grocery store on the banks of the Erie Canal in the community of Fort Herkimer in the early 1900s. They were longtime residents there, attending the nearby Fort Herkimer Church. (Courtesy of Ann Casler Green.)

STORE MOVED TO THE HIGHWAY. Changes were coming with the construction of the new Barge Canal, and in 1909, Ella and Hawley Casler received a summons that their land was being appropriated for the use of the canals. In 1911, they purchased land from Carrie Strobel near the Fort Herkimer Church and moved their store to the highway there. Pictured in front of the grocery when it was on the canal is their son Arthur Casler on the left. (Courtesy of Ann Casler Green.)

ILION MARINA. The Ilion Marina, the first marina in Herkimer County, was opened in May 1961 with over 100 spectators present. A 12-boat flotilla left Sylvan Beach with dignitaries who arrived at the new marina for dedication ceremonies conducted by Malvin Applegate, president of the Ilion Chamber of Commerce. Today the marina is enjoyed by many people who boat on the canal or by leisurely fishermen sitting on its banks.

A VIEW ENTERING ILION. This view of Ilion was taken in the early 1900s before the 1912 Presbyterian church fire and before the four-lane Route 5 and the overpasses of today. The Clarke and Baker Company's factory, seen on the far right, was taken over by Library Bureau. Right next to it is Chismore Park, named after Henry Chismore, who owned the land. The park had a harness racing track, stables for the horses, a baseball field, and a picnic area. (Courtesy of IL.)

RAILROAD STREET BRIDGE. Railroad Street Bridge, shown around 1890, was Ilion's busiest canal intersection. Note the high embankments on either end of the bridge. This was done to allow the canal boats to pass under. At the left center of the photograph is the Central Hotel, which fronted on Railroad Street (Central Avenue) and Canal Street. Farther back and more to the right is the Remington Typewriter Works. (Courtesy of Remington Arms.)

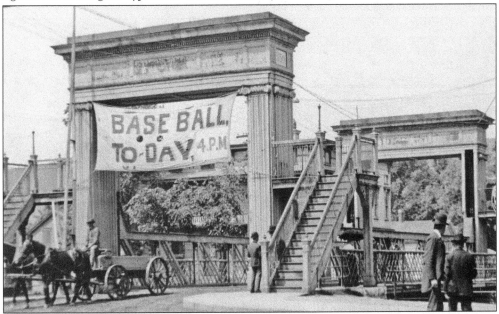

LIFT BRIDGE IN ILION. This lift bridge, constructed in 1897, replaced the Railroad Street Bridge and was the last bridge constructed over the Erie Canal in Ilion. It was an electric marvel in its day. Steel cables on revolving drums raised and lowered the structure in accordance with the bridge tender's manipulation. The banner announcing "Baseball Today" confirms Ilion's dedication to the game and their baseball team, the Clippers. (Courtesy of IL.)

SWIMMING MEET ON THE BRIDGE. A swimming meet at the lift bridge can be seen in this 1912 photograph. Crowds would gather to watch men dive from the steel girders. Seen across the canal is the business area of Main Street, including Powers Wine and Liquors. The stairs to the lift bridge were removed in 1920, and the bridge itself was torn down in 1924, three years after the canal was abandoned. (Courtesy of Tim Daly.)

ALL ROADS LEAD TO MOHAWK. All the modes of transportation in Mohawk are represented in this c. 1920 photograph. Broad Street, with its pedestrian walkway, approaches the bridges to Herkimer, paralleled by the electric trolley line, while Route 5S is barely visible behind the West Shore Railroad tracks. In the lower right can be seen both the old Erie Canal and the new Barge Canal alongside the Mohawk River. The buildings of Herkimer National Desk Company can be seen in the background.

AERIAL VIEW ENTERING MOHAWK. The intersection of Broad Street and Route 5S has changed dramatically in this 1982 photograph. Gone is any trace of the Erie Canal, now covered by Route 5S. The West Shore Railroad bed can be seen at the lower left, although its rails and overpass bridge are gone. The intersection is now dominated by Carparelli Brothers (building supplies) and Bull Brothers gas station.

AERIAL VIEW OF DOWNTOWN MOHAWK. This 1961 photograph showing the intersection of Main and Columbia Streets in Mohawk gives a bird's-eye view of downtown. The Mobil gas station on the corner of Columbia and Main Streets is visible. Next to it is Jarvis Pharmacy. Further up at the corner of Washington Street is the Oneida National Bank. On the other side of the street near Warren Street is Mohawk Hardware and Plumbing, and on the corner of Otsego Street is Cook's Variety.

Visit us at
arcadiapublishing.com

Printed in the USA
CPSIA information can be obtained
at www.ICGtesting.com
LVHW081957171123
764248LV00009B/837